W9-BWT-773

GIVING AWAY SUCCESS

WHY WOMEN GET STUCK AND WHAT TO DO ABOUT IT

GIVING AWAY SUCCESS

WHY WOMEN GET STUCK
AND WHAT TO DO ABOUT IT

REVISED EDITION
Susan Schenkel, Ph.D.

HarperPerennial
A Division of HarperCollinsPublishers

A hardcover edition of this book was originally published in 1984 by McGraw-Hill. The revised edition was previously published in 1991 by Random House, Inc. It is here reprinted by arrangement with Random House, Inc.

GIVING AWAY SUCCESS (Revised Edition). Copyright © 1984, 1991 by Susan Schenkel, Ph.D. All rights reserved. Printed in the United States of America. No part of this book may be used or reproduced in any manner whatsoever without written permission except in the case of brief quotations embodied in critical articles and reviews. For information address HarperCollins Publishers, Inc., 10 East 53rd Street, New York, NY 10022.

HarperCollins books may be purchased for educational, business, or sales promotional use. For information, please call or write: Special Markets Department, HarperCollins Publishers, Inc., 10 East 53rd Street, New York, NY 10022. Telephone: (212) 207-7528; Fax: (212) 207-7222.

First HarperPerennial edition published 1992.

Library of Congress Cataloging-in-Publication Data

Schenkel, Susan.
  Giving away success: why women get stuck and what to do about it / Susan Schenkel. — Rev. ed.
    p.   cm.
  Previously published : New York : Random House, 1991.
  Includes bibliographical references and index.
  ISBN 0-06-097460-5 (pbk.)
  1. Women — Psychology. 2. Self-confidence. 3. Failure (Psychology). 4. Assertiveness (Psychology). I. Title.
  HQ1206.S38   1992   91-55470
  155.6'33—dc20

92 93 94 95 96 RRD 10 9 8 7 6 5 4 3 2 1

*To my parents, Leon and Siddi
Schenkel, who taught me that a
woman has to be able to make her
own way in the world*

and

*To my husband, Alvin Helfeld,
who gave me love and support and
read every draft of every chapter.*

Preface

THROUGHOUT my twenty-year career as a psychologist, I have been involved with women's issues, and for the past decade I have been particularly fascinated by the subject of women and action. That is, why motivated women have difficulty taking action and what can be done about it. My interest in this topic produced *Giving Away Success*, which was published in 1984.

Since its publication many women have shared with me—in workshops, counseling sessions, and letters—their thoughts about being stuck. Feedback from women of all ages, occupations, educational levels, and backgrounds has supported the validity and usefulness of the concepts and self-help strategies derived from behavioral psychology. It has been very gratifying to find that the ideas have held up over time. However, as I continue to work in this area, I realize that certain ideas and strategies warrant more attention.

The dizzying changes in the world and in the workplace have convinced me that it's more important than ever that women be able to take effective action. Since thriving in the new environment of global competition will require a high level of initiative, it's crucial that women overcome their internal barriers to taking action. This conviction has motivated me to present my new ideas in a revised and expanded edition of *Giving Away Success*. Because the response to the first book was so informative and inspiring,

I believe I have been able to improve it. Many thanks to all of you for your help and enthusiasm. May you seek success and find it.

Cambridge, Massachusetts
June 1990

Acknowledgments

I WOULD like to thank the many people who shared their experiences and who encouraged this project. In particular, I would like to express my gratitude to Dr. Linda Silver, Dr. Marie Guzell, Dr. Margaret Lloyd, Dr. Siddi Schenkel, Eliza McCormack, Mary Oates Johnson, and Alvin Helfeld for their perceptive comments on the manuscript and their support.

In addition, I would like to thank publisher Joni Evans for her faith in the book, and executive editor Susan Kamil for her extremely sensitive editing and her enthusiasm.

Contents

"I want to, but I can't get myself to . . ."

Several years ago, a thirty-three-year-old woman named Charlotte came to counseling presenting the following problem:

I have a small business. Several steady accounts provide me with a somewhat marginal existence. I want more work but I am not doing enough to get new accounts. I am afraid that my business is going to fall apart unless I take some action.

There is a lot I could do but I just don't do it. I know my ideas are good and that they would pan out if I followed through on them, but I can't seem to find the initiative. Sometimes I even have trouble getting through some of the routine stuff: phone calls don't get returned promptly, bills don't get sent out, reports don't get written. My distress keeps growing but it doesn't propel me into action. If anything, it makes it harder for me to get into gear.

I don't want to talk about my love life or my childhood. I want to save my business. Can you help me?

Charlotte's problem started me thinking. I had worked with women who had had similar difficulties: an aspiring actress who couldn't get herself to auditions; a professional writer who didn't take advantage of opportunities that fell into her lap; a lab technician who hated her job but couldn't get herself to look for another. The essence of all these problems was "I want to, but I can't get myself to . . ."

Up to this point, I had thought about these women as people with individual problems. But as I thought about it more, similarities began to appear. As I put these patterns into the broader context of the psychology of women, it occurred to me that the problem was a women's issue: Intelligent, talented women felt blocked from achievement by internal obstacles that they could barely articulate, much less understand.

When I thought about it further, I realized there was a consistent pattern to the strategies I used to help people who were stuck. Strangely enough, though, I had much clearer ideas about the solution than I did about the problem. My grasp of situations had been highly intuitive and, like my clients, I didn't have well-articulated concepts to help organize my thinking. The standard formulations, such as fear of success, identity confusion, anxiety, and depression, weren't satisfying.

I set about to conceptualize what gets women stuck

and to organize helpful strategies for getting unstuck. As I reviewed a broad range of theory, research, and case material, the goal I set for myself was to describe the problems in a practical way, in a manner that had clear implications for change. I didn't want to write yet another book that described women's dilemmas and then left the reader thinking, "Well, now what?"

The strategies and techniques for getting unstuck, derived from my clinical experience and from a field of psychology called behavioral self-management, consist of a variety of simple, uncomplicated activities that help people get moving and manage their own behavior more effectively. The examples I have used to illustrate them, although disguised to insure confidentiality, come from the lives of real people.

The problems described in this book aren't unique to women. Men have them too. But there is a difference. Because men's socialization has traditionally encouraged achievement, fewer men than women have difficulty taking action in the arena of work. When men do get stuck, it isn't because society has systematically discouraged their achievement.

On the other hand, motivated women who have difficulty taking action usually have a great deal in common, despite individual differences. Many of their issues are totally predictable. These communalities are the basis of this book. They exist because the predisposition to get stuck is the legacy of growing up female. The confining conditions of traditional femininity have created, for many of us, internal barriers to achievement.

Although some features of women's reality are disheartening, this book is written in optimism. My wish is to share this optimism and to bring hope and a sense of empowerment to those who read the book.

Part One

GETTING STUCK

CHAPTER 1

Why Women Lack Confidence

A dream come true. Ann noticed her hands trembling as she put down the receiver. She had just been offered a wonderful job. The job of a lifetime: challenging, well paying, with plenty of opportunity to meet interesting people. Now it had happened and she was terrified. She couldn't possibly do it. She didn't know enough. She wasn't poised enough. She wasn't shrewd enough. She had fooled them. The interviews were theatrical performances that could have won an Oscar. Her résumé was a lot of clever words artfully strung together on fancy paper. She had good references only because people liked her. She couldn't really do the job, though, could she?

Ann's doubts and fears are common to many women. We question our intelligence, talent, and skill. We wonder about the value of our ideas and actions. We have trouble taking ourselves seriously, finding it hard to believe our talents warrant full expression and recognition. We minimize our accomplishments. All this in the face of excellent track records.

A major reason for our lack of confidence is that we, as women, learn to view our abilities in the same way that society views them. Traditional sex role stereotypes portray women as emotional, helpless, and intuitive; whereas men are portrayed as rational, competent, and smart. For women competence is a questionable asset at best. Being brainy is downright unfeminine. Achievement, assertion, and aggression belong squarely in the male domain.

Out of the mouths of babes comes society's conventional notions about women and men. In a research study, interviewers asked two thousand schoolchildren one question: "If you woke up tomorrow and discovered you were a (boy) (girl), how would your life be different?"[1]

The responses revealed what researchers called "a fundamental contempt for females." For example, elementary school boys often titled their answers with phrases such as "Doomsday," and then went on to describe how terrible their lives would be if they were girls. A sixth-grade boy wrote, "If I were a girl, I'd be stupid and weak as a string." A teenaged boy wrote, "If I were a girl, I would use a lot of makeup and look good and beautiful to everyone, knowing that few people would care for my personality." And when boys even considered the possibility that as women they could work outside the home, the jobs they listed most often were nurse and secretary.

Girls, on the other hand, wrote that if they were boys they would be better off. In the words of one eleventh-grade girl, "People would take my decisions and beliefs more seriously." A tenth-grader wrote, "If I were a boy, I think I would be more outspoken and confident, but I really don't know why." Boys thought that being a girl would be confining, and girls thought that being a boy would be liberating.

Sex role stereotypes get instilled early in life. They form the content of the rules we use to judge social behavior. These rules become part of our daily thinking habits, and our judgments become so automatic we hardly notice them.

As a result of learning society's prejudices against women's competence, many women become prejudiced against their own competence. They learn to judge themselves according to rules that reflect a negative bias against their abilities. The logic of these rules goes something like this: (1) women don't have much ability; (2) since I am a woman, I don't have much ability; (3) therefore I can't have high expectations of success—particularly in those areas specifically identified as masculine; (4) if success comes my way, it must be attributed to something other than ability.

This devastating logic becomes embedded in women's thinking and expresses itself in women's evaluations of their actions.

THE FEMININE DISCOUNTING HABIT

Sally, a woman in her late twenties, was enrolled in a high-powered Master's of Business Administration program. In her marketing course, the class was divided into teams for a market research project. As it happened, all six members of Sally's team were women. They worked very hard. They spent evenings and weekends doing research and discussing their findings. They wrote and rewrote. After weeks of preparation, they presented their project to the entire class.

It was a big success. The material was thoroughly researched and well organized. The speakers were poised and articulate. They handled questions with assurance and competence. Their professor and fellow classmates gave them rave reviews, the best presentation in the class.

Oddly enough, Sally's teammates didn't pay much attention to their success. In fact, they took great pains to belittle it: "It wasn't really that good," "There was a mistake here; they overlooked this and forgot that," "The rest of the class didn't really try that hard."

In deprecating their accomplishment, Sally's team was undermining the very success they were working so hard to achieve. These bright, talented, ambitious women were unwittingly violating one of the cardinal rules of success: Accentuate the positive, eliminate the negative. One can hardly imagine the (male) board of directors of a *Fortune* 500 company discrediting record-breaking corporate profits.

Unfortunately, Sally's story isn't an isolated incident. Far too many of us sell ourselves short by discrediting, minimizing, belittling, and devaluing our abilities and accomplishments. Research, as well as common observation, documents this tendency. When women and men were asked to evaluate their own performance, women frequently deprecated the quality of their product.[2] Even when their work was identical to that of their male counterparts, women rated it less favorably.

This tendency toward negative self-evaluation emerged in another study as well. Girls and boys were given a task to perform and then were given mixed messages about their performance.[3] Some of the time they were told they had done well, and at other times they were told they hadn't. How did the children evaluate their efforts? The girls tended to focus on the negative feedback and conclude they had done poorly, while the boys focused on the positive feedback and concluded they had done well.

Focusing on the negative while ignoring the positive was Marie's first response to an invitation to run for town council. She had grown up in a politically active family. Her father was a union leader, and her older brother, a lawyer, was involved in state politics. Marie herself had worked on political campaigns since high school. She loved politics and understood the workings of power. But when she was asked to be a candidate, she froze. Her immediate reaction was to catalog all her weaknesses: all the things she didn't know, her unpredictable periods of self-doubt, and her panic at surprise attacks. Only later, after some counseling, did she focus on her strengths: her intelligence, articulateness, political savvy, popularity, and sincere desire to improve her hometown.

Like Marie, we all have strengths and weaknesses, and we all receive both positive and negative feedback. When we transform mixed reviews into negative ones, when we focus exclusively on our weaknesses, we get an inaccurate picture of ourselves. We develop an unfavorable self-image that keeps us from taking action. Marie's negative outlook might have discouraged her from running for office. Fortunately, in time she saw the total picture and decided to run. But many women never get past the negative to see a more balanced and realistic picture of themselves, and they never get going.

When it's impossible to ignore positive feedback, we can discount ourselves by automatically attributing our success to something other than ability. Jane, a Ph.D. in psychology, thought she was lucky when she passed the licensing exam. Carol figured it was a fluke when she was accepted to law school. Diane, a research assistant in a university laboratory, was afraid to look for a new job because she thought her current success was due to luck. Elaine, finding herself district manager, attributed it to political events beyond her control—being in the right place at the right time.

It's tempting to regard "luck" as a figure of speech. But it's a *woman's* figure of speech. Research tells us that while men tend to attribute their success to ability, women tend to attribute their success to luck rather than skill.[4]

When we automatically attribute our success to luck, we deny our ability. We transform ourselves from active participants to passive recipients. We lose our sense of control and competence.

How many times have we heard a woman say, "Oh, it was nothing"? This offhand remark captures the essence of another common form of discounting: attributing success to the simplicity of the task. "When things come easy to me, I think they are simple, not that I am smart," observed one woman. Another remarked, "I tend to think that things are easy, and that people should be able to do them. So I don't get impressed with myself for doing them."

Underneath these seemingly innocuous comments is an insidious logic that goes like this: (1) since I am not particularly intelligent or competent, I can't do difficult things; (2) it follows that if I can do something, it must be easy. This reasoning begins with questionable assumptions from which follow questionable conclusions. When the basic assumptions are wrong, which they often are, we discount our abilities and accomplishments.

Some women, particularly older women, discount themselves by attributing their own success to the efforts of others. "Giving away success" embodies some of the basic canons of traditional femininity: putting others first, self-sacrifice, and modesty. Those who take this to the extreme won't take credit for *any* success. Janet, a forty-eight-year-old wife and mother, is such a person. A woman with remarkable organizational skill, Janet volunteers her time to her church and a school for retarded children. But whether she organizes a bake sale or a children's play, she never takes the credit. Janet was just lending a helping hand. "I didn't do anything, really," is one of her stock phrases. She doesn't acknowledge to herself or to anyone else the extent of her accomplishments.

Giving away success is facilitated by a related habit of building up others at one's own expense. Janet routinely exaggerates everyone's brains and talents. Her world is filled with people who are more intelligent and creative than she could ever hope to be. Her friend's diploma is bona fide proof that he is a dynamic genius bound for glory; her diploma is suitable for wrapping fish.

A far more subtle method of discounting our abilities is to attribute our success to hard work. In a research study, men and women managers were asked to account for their success.[5] Men felt that hard work and ability were equally important. Women, however, attributed their success only to hard work. Ability didn't even enter the picture. Surely no one can be faulted for attributing success to hard work. That's as American as apple pie. But attributing success *entirely* to effort leaves out an important ingredient: skill. After all, oxen work hard but they don't get six-figure salaries or Nobel prizes.

In accounting for success, it's often easier for women to acknowledge endearing personality characteristics than to acknowledge ability. A female law student won a plum, a clerkship at the state supreme judicial court. A thousand people had applied for the sixteen positions available. Yet when someone complimented her on her coup, she dismissed it by saying, "Oh, that was no coup, I just happened to charm the judge." In a similar example, a teacher working in one of the best high schools in Massachusetts was praising the brilliance of her colleagues. But in talking about her own work she focused on her inadequacies. When asked to account for her long tenure at such an excellent school, she replied, "I'm enthusiastic. I got the job and have kept it because of my personality." This high school teacher, like the law clerk, felt free to acknowledge her personality because charm is consistent with the traditional female role. Women are supposed to be delightful. And, in fact, charm is a great asset in work relationships. But it's the icing on the cake. Without intelligence, talent, and skill, charm will go only so far.

All these automatic attributions—luck, easy tasks, efforts of others, hard work, and charm—keep us from reflecting on our actions and appreciating our abilities and accomplishments. They keep us from experiencing ourselves as competent and talented. That's a big loss.

Not only do women readily attribute their success to something other than ability, they are quick to blame their failures on lack of ability. Barbara, a thirty-six-year-old woman with a doctorate in education, teaches part-time in a community college. In addition, she runs a small consulting business and writes articles for professional journals. Despite her accomplishments, when Barbara doesn't succeed at something, she automatically assumes that she lacks ability. Once she spent an entire weekend juggling around numbers that just wouldn't come out right. Finally, in sheer desperation, she presented the problem to her husband, fully expecting him to solve it in five minutes. She was genuinely amazed when, after two hours, he too gave up.

Barbara wasn't crazy. She was simply doing what women frequently do when confronted with failure. She assumed she lacked ability. Although there are many ways to account for failure—lack of effort, lack of information, bad luck, or an impossible task—research tells us that women frequently use lack of ability as their explanation.[6] Men rarely do so.

A businesswoman summed it up: "I get myself coming and going. I blame myself for my failures and I don't give myself credit for my successes."

On the face of it, these attribution patterns appear self-defeating. And they are. But we are just doing what we have been taught to do. Society makes attributions on the basis of sex role stereotypes and we learn this "reasoning" process. We apply it to our own behavior as well as to the behavior of others.

Research has demonstrated that people evaluate each other on the basis of sex role stereotypes. In one study, participants were asked to judge whether a person's performance was due primarily to skill or to luck.[7] Although the performances were identical, the judges tended to use skill to account for men's performances and luck to account for women's. In a similar experiment, participants were asked to account for the success or failure of either a male or female graduate student.[8] Again, the man's success was attributed to ability, while the woman's success was attributed to luck, easy courses, and even to cheating. By the same token, the woman's failure was blamed on lack of ability more often than was the man's.

In some cases, luck is out of the question. For example, participants in another study were asked to account for the success of either Dr. Marcia Greer or Dr. Mark Greer.[9] The judges tended to say that Dr. Marcia's success was a result of effort while Dr. Mark's success was a result of ability.

The participants in these studies judged women in the same way that women judge themselves. Ability, skill, competence, and achievement belong to the male preserve and don't fit the traditional image of women. So when women are successful, it must be explained in some other way. Luck or effort can account for success without doing violence to traditional notions about the nature of masculinity and femininity. Ability is kept firmly in the male domain.

Such social judgments don't happen only in psychology experiments. Recently, at a cocktail party, I overheard snatches of a conversation between two women getting acquainted. One was a highly successful professional woman and the other was a wife and mother who works part-time. The professional woman said she was teaching at Harvard, to which the other woman replied, "How lucky for you." A spontaneous remark made without any apparent malice: an echo of our culture.

A more subtle example: Rosalie, a bright and competent woman, quickly worked her way up from secretary to assistant to the dean in a small liberal arts college. The dean was pleased with her work and said he wanted to help her advance, but for several years nothing happened.

One day Rosalie received a written performance evaluation and noticed something intriguing about the sentence structure. When the dean discussed her weaknesses, he used the active voice: "Rosalie is often late." But when he discussed her strengths, he used the passive voice: "Functions organized by Rosalie always run smoothly." Instead of stating clearly that Rosalie was a good organizer, the dean was suggesting that things "happened to" Rosalie, that she was the recipient of good fortune whereby events flowed smoothly around her. One might conclude that Rosalie was a lucky rather than a skillful administrator.

IMPACT

The feminine discounting habit deprives us of positive feedback. When we are focusing on the negative, discrediting success, or blaming imagined incompetence, we are not paying attention to what we did well and how we did it. It's as if our brain were a computer with loose wires. Instead of registering "success," the computer rejects the information: "Will not compute!"

Let's take an example. Suppose you think that auto mechanics is beyond the realm of comprehension. You don't know a radiator from a carburetor. If anything goes wrong, the chances of your fixing it are pretty slim. Now imagine being stranded on a deserted road with a flat tire. The man with you has a broken arm and can't change the tire. All he can do is give you instructions. So he talks and you work. When you are finished, you go on your way. Your worst nightmares don't come true: the car doesn't collapse, and the tire doesn't blow out. You arrive at your destination safe and sound, no worse for wear. How do you think about your experience?

You could think: "I learned how to change a tire and

I can do it again if I have to. I have more mechanical ability than I thought." Or, you could think: "I sure am lucky that I wasn't alone. It would have been a disaster. I am so hopeless with cars."

If you think the latter, you discount your accomplishment. Yes, it was fortunate that someone was available to teach you when you needed help. But instead of focusing on what you learned and the fact that you—no one else—changed the tire, you are focusing on feelings of helplessness prior to learning.

There are consequences of ignoring feedback. First, positive feedback tells us what works. It tells us what type of behavior is effective and that we have the ability to execute this effective behavior. If we can do something once, it's likely we can do it again—and also likely that we can be successful in similar activities. This knowledge allows us to anticipate success in the future.

When we don't integrate positive feedback, we lack the information that permits us to be optimistic about future endeavors. This prevents us from modifying unrealistically low expectations and increasing our self-confidence.

Experiencing success helps us develop a psychological buffer against life's inevitable failures. The sting of any particular failure hurts less when we can look back at past successes and anticipate future achievement. We see failure as a temporary setback rather than an omen of inescapable doom, and we bounce back more easily.

But when our successes don't register there is no protective layer around our self-esteem. Like a bad cold, thoughts of failure settle in and hang on too long. As one woman put it, "I can chew on a mistake forever."

When positive feedback isn't absorbed, we lose more than crucial information and psychological protection. We are deprived of happy thoughts and good feelings as well. When we ignore our accomplishments, we miss the chance to feel good and reward ourselves. As a result, we are less

likely to find achievement gratifying, and may be less inclined to pursue it. One woman put it this way, "When I
think of where I started out, I know it's a major accomplishment. I know that intellectually. But I don't stop to
congratulate myself and really enjoy it. That may be why
I don't actively seek out more accomplishments and
successes."

If we don't congratulate and celebrate ourselves, we
must look elsewhere for validation. This makes us more
dependent on others for recognition and approval.

Ironically, the very discounting habit that makes us
more needy of recognition and approval from others interferes with our getting them. In order to obtain these psychological rewards, as well as the tangible rewards of money
and privilege, we must *claim* them. But that's exactly what
we have trouble doing when we are unconvinced of our
worth. Discounting leads to lack of self-assertion, which in
turn decreases our chances of being rewarded.

This is apparent in the problem many women have in
dealing with money. Requesting raises, negotiating salaries,
setting fees, demanding payment—all these can be nightmares for women who are unconvinced of their worth.
Imagine the dilemma of a consultant in the fast-track field
of finance who said, "I have trouble setting fees. I feel
embarrassed to ask for so much money. I think to myself,
'Who am I to be asking for this?' It's really a problem
because clients tend to think that high fees mean high quality. You know, the 'you get what you pay for' mentality."

When we minimize our ability, we are less likely to
make a commitment to it. It doesn't make sense to do so.
Why take the risks, make the sacrifices, and work like a
dog for third-rate talent and questionable results? In such
a way, the feminine discounting habit becomes yet another
voice arguing against women's pursuit of their talents.

Even when we do make commitments, it's a psychological juggling act to simultaneously discount ourselves

and take effective action. The discrepancy between our self-image and our activities causes confusion and anxiety. Will the real Ann Jones please stand up? Is she the poised businesswoman at the podium or the terrified creature hoping to become invisible? Ann Jones doesn't know! And this confusion creates a sense of fraudulence. Trying to project a positive image in the face of disbelief makes one feel like an imposter. Recall Ann's reaction to the offer of her dream job. She believed she had deceived people into thinking she could conquer the world, when, in fact, she felt like an incompetent nobody. Another woman summed up her experience by saying, "I feel like a kid forging a note."

In censoring positive feedback, the feminine discounting habit distorts our perception of success and failure and discredits our abilities and accomplishments. It shrinks our self-image and our horizons, closing off interesting, rewarding, and lucrative activities. The psychological, social, and economic costs are enormous. Women who sell themselves short pay a high price.

CHAPTER 2

Feeling Helpless

I quit," she said. "I just gave up. I have been spending my days baking bread and reading Harlequin romances. I haven't tried to look for work in months. I don't even think about it much. My friends are all doing the same thing."

Feeling helpless is what brought twenty-seven-year-old Nora Johnson to counseling. Her current state was a shock to her. Until fairly recently, her life had proceeded predictably.

Brought up traditionally, Nora had gone to college to find a husband. While she searched, she majored in elementary education. It was the obvious choice: she liked children and everyone had said, "Teaching is such a good profession for a woman." The arguments in favor of it had seemed compelling. It provided pleasant work, job security, and plenty of vacation time. Best of all, when she had her own children, she could continue working without taking too much time away from them. True, the salary wasn't enormous. But that wasn't important for a woman: someone would always take care of her.

According to plan, Nora met Bill and they got married after graduation. Shrewd, ambitious, and energetic, Bill saw his future in high technology. He took a job with a computer company in Massachusetts and Nora followed. She found a job teaching in a local elementary school. She liked her work and her colleagues and she loved her summers off. All in all, it was a good life.

One day the roof fell in. The citizens of Massachusetts decided they were fed up and weren't going to take it anymore. The government would have to eliminate waste and trim its budget. A tax revolt was at hand. Education was hit hard. Many teachers lost their jobs, and Nora was one of them.

With one blow, she lost her job, her salary, her career, a big piece of her identity, and her life-style. Having believed she was set for life, she suddenly found herself cast adrift with no anchor or sense of direction.

Bill said there was money in sales and actively encouraged her to move in that direction. Obligingly, Nora set up an interview. It bombed. The interviewer made her wait for half an hour and when he finally got around to seeing her, his manner was arrogant and patronizing. She felt intimidated and acted, as she put it, "disgustingly ingratiating and mealymouthed." It was a disaster from start to finish.

In the months that followed, Nora made a few haphazard attempts at finding a job. Then she stopped looking. She responded to her situation with helplessness: She threw up her hands and threw in the towel.

We experience helplessness when we think there is little or nothing we can do to influence events. It's a psychological state in which we may feel some degree of emotional distress and think thoughts such as "What's the point?" and "It's useless to try." All these thoughts have a common theme: "I can't do it."

Helpless thoughts are often followed by helpless behavior. The essence is noninvolvement, in either of two basic forms. The first is premature withdrawal: stopping, quitting, or escaping before making exhaustive attempts to solve existing problems. That's what Nora did. She stopped her job hunt long before objective circumstances warranted such a retreat. The second is avoidance. If withdrawal is getting out of a tight spot, avoidance is steering clear of it in the first place. Avoidance can be almost any type of behavior that effectively spares us—in the short run—from confrontation with difficulties we feel unable or unwilling to handle. Nora used baking and reading to distract herself from the responsibility of looking for work. She was able to avoid, a good deal of the time, both the stress of looking for a new job and the distress involved in facing up to her inertia.

Like Nora, those of us who feel stuck tend to respond helplessly at critical points. We have learned to avoid and withdraw, either as a response to specific career challenges or as a general response to life's stresses.

Understanding helplessness and how it develops gives valuable insight into why people get stuck. Psychologist Martin Seligman has made a great contribution to our knowledge by developing a theory that is based on scientific laboratory research. Dr. Seligman and his colleagues studied the relationship between fear and learning in animals. In one experiment, dogs were placed in a chamber and subjected to moderately painful shocks that they could not avoid or escape.[1] They could howl and wriggle and run around, but nothing they did could prevent or stop the shocks. Objectively, the dogs were in an *uncontrollable* situation.

In the next experiment, the conditions were changed. The dogs could escape the shocks by jumping over a barrier placed in the middle of the chamber. This situation was potentially *controllable* if they could figure out what to do. Helplessness wasn't inevitable.

A new group of dogs quickly learned to jump over the barrier. But the "old" dogs—those subjected to uncontrollable shocks in the first study—behaved very differently in the new situation. After a brief and frantic run around the chamber, they just lay down. On subsequent trials, they didn't even try; they passively tolerated the shocks. In striking contrast to the new dogs, the old ones never learned to escape the shocks. They behaved in a helpless manner when, in reality, they could have taken control. Dr. Seligman calls this *learned helplessness*.[2]

What do shocked dogs have to do with looking for a job, applying to law school, or feeling confident? Very simply, some of us function like Seligman's traumatized dogs: We feel and act helpless when in fact we aren't. We have learned helplessness.

Since helplessness is a major theme in the lives of many women, this research sheds light on those lives. The study of animals makes an important point: All creatures who lack control over their environment can learn helplessness. Women's helplessness isn't an innately and uniquely feminine characteristic; it's a predictable response to social conditions.

LEARNING HELPLESSNESS

If atmospheric conditions call for rain, it will rain. We can dance, pray, or cry over a ruined picnic, but we can't change the weather. This reality, which objectively exists in the world, is what Dr. Seligman calls *uncontrollability*.[3]

We can experience uncontrollable events, such as the weather, directly. We can also learn of their existence from any credible authority. When we believe a person who tells us "It can't be done," irrespective of the accuracy of that statement, we experience an uncontrollable situation. Or, to put it another way, we can be taught helplessness despite potentially controllable circumstances. As we shall see, the fact that uncontrollability can be taught by others has serious implications for women.

Uncontrollability creates the perception that nothing can be done to influence the outcome of events. Learned helplessness is the consequence of transferring this perception from an uncontrollable situation to a new or changed situation where it may not apply. Learned helplessness is an *assumption* based on an overgeneralization from previous experience. If it walks like a duck and quacks like a duck, we assume it's a duck. Having made this assumption, we don't stop to notice that the "duck" doesn't like water and can't swim, and that our guess is wrong.

The old dogs made this type of mistake. Due to their initial exposure to inescapable shock, they lost their ability to discriminate. When the rules changed and the situation became controllable, they didn't see it. They continued to behave as if they were in the chamber of unavoidable shocks. When their first attempt to escape failed, this confirmed their assumption of helplessness and they gave up. They never found out that with a few more tries they could have been home free.

Uncontrollable circumstances distorted the dogs' perceptions and disrupted their ability to tell the difference between what could and could not be controlled. They saw "impossible" where they could have seen "possible." As a result, they underestimated their powers and acted helpless.

Many of us are in the same boat. Having been brought up with traditional femininity, in a world full of Stop and No Trespassing signs, we acquired a relatively limited notion of what is possible. And while these social realities are, admittedly, more controllable than the weather, they do create their own uncontrollable conditions.

Certain realms of endeavor and types of behavior were regarded as "male." These were off-limits; no women need apply. For all the control we could expect to exert, these masculine strongholds might as well have been filled with starving lions, erupting volcanoes, and falling meteorites. Mastery of them was clearly beyond us.

Then the world turned and the scene shifted. "Going to college to marry a lawyer only to find out at graduation she was supposed to be one" is how playwright Wendy Wasserstein summed up the problem. Leaving the confinement of exclusively female roles, we moved on to wider opportunities in male domains. The rules were changing. The uncontrollable conditions in "experiment one" were becoming controllable in "experiment two."

Although playing a new scene, many of us are still reading our old lines. While intellectually understanding the changing role of women, in daily behavior our perceptions are conditioned by the old regime. Too much looks uncontrollable. We don't appreciate the ways in which we can exercise power.

Society's new demands for different types of competence haven't created learned helplessness. They have merely made the existing problem more apparent. The causes of learned helplessness are all the experiences that teach us that we lack ability and the power to control.

A Classic Example: Math Anxiety

"My mind goes blank every time I see numbers," said a fifty-year-old woman who had recently completed a doctorate in French literature. "When I took the Graduate Record Exam to get into graduate school, I placed in the ninety-eighth percentile in the humanities and in the second percentile in math. I just assumed I couldn't do it."

This woman is in good company. A university professor observed that many of his female students suffered from mental blocks in learning statistics.[4] A social worker, who was also a mathematician, made similar observations when interviewing graduate students and mental health professionals.[5] He found that these women, high achievers in other areas, responded to math-related activities with symptoms usually associated with phobias. A case in point is a thirty-three-year-old social worker who describes her feelings this way: "I can't stand to add my checkbook. I hate it. I get anxious as hell. I avoid it . . . it's crazy. I get nauseous. . . . There was something about math—about numbers. My thinking would get clouded. The anxiety would overwhelm me and I would get terrified that it wouldn't come out right. . . . I can memorize other things, but when it came to math I couldn't memorize it if I didn't understand it."[6]

These women didn't lose some of their intellectual functioning due to brain damage. They were taught helplessness by a culture that defined math as belonging to the male domain, as something that women could never expect to master.

Despite evidence to the contrary, both teachers and students accept this cultural assumption.[7] When boys do poorly in math in high school and college, they attribute it to insufficient effort. On the other hand, girls who fail are three times more likely to attribute failure to lack of ability.

Women are taught to believe that this presumed inferiority is normal. Conventional stereotypes convey the notion that math is unfeminine. A real woman wouldn't want to bother her pretty little head with all those complicated symbols any more than she would want to dig a ditch.

The relationship between traditional role expectations and helplessness was demonstrated dramatically in a study of several hundred seventh- and eighth-grade girls.[8] Knowing a girl's attitude toward conformity to traditional female role expectations would enable one to predict her level of achievement in math. By and large, those girls who conformed to traditional expectations were low achievers, while those who rebelled against them were high achievers.

Math anxiety is a vivid example of the blurring of the distinction between what we are told we shouldn't do and what we are told we can't do. With a sleight of hand, the culture has translated "shouldn't" into "can't." Those of us plagued with math anxiety have accepted this equation as valid. We believe we lack ability when what we really lack is society's unequivocal permission to use whatever talent we possess.

Although society has given us many lessons on our lack of ability and power to control, times are changing. The forces of history are creating new opportunities, and women are exploring uncharted terrain. The limits of the possibilities are far from clear. They vary according to field, geographic location, social customs, personalities, and various intangibles. Conditions are changing daily. What was true yesterday may not be true tomorrow.

In this constantly changing landscape, our perceptions are a critical force. A sense of optimism about our ability to have impact and influence our environment will allow us to perceive the sometimes subtle changes that create new opportunities. Our success may very well depend on our ability to make these fine discriminations. Learned helplessness impairs this ability and makes prospects look needlessly bleak.

IMPACT

Learned helplessness has devastating effects on behavior: (1) it destroys motivation, (2) it interferes with the ability to learn, and (3) it creates emotional distress.

Lost Motivation

"Nothing in the world can take the place of persistence. Talent will not; nothing is more common than unsuccessful men with talent. Genius will not; unrewarded genius is almost a proverb. Education will not; the world is full of educated derelicts. Persistence and determination alone are omnipotent!"[9]

In the face of learned helplessness, initiative dies on the vine. Persistence wilts. If we believe our efforts are futile, we take less action. When we do act, we tend to give up if we don't have immediate success.

We have seen this passivity in Seligman's dogs. Research with people obtained comparable results.[10] Psychologists subjected a group of college students to a loud, irritating, uncontrollable noise; a second group was able to stop the noise by pressing a button; a third group heard no noise. In the second phase of the study, all three groups were subjected to noise they could learn to escape by moving their fingers back and forth in a box. Like the old dogs, the college students who had been subjected to the uncontrollable situation behaved passively. They just sat and listened to the blare. Unlike the students in the other two groups, who learned to escape the noise, they didn't try and they never learned how.

Intelligence, talent, and skill are held hostage to learned helplessness. By narrowing our vision of what is possible, it restrains imagination and lowers aspirations.

Motivational problems appear all over the landscape of women's lives. Lack of initiative and persistence can be spotted in so-called laziness, work inhibitions, apathy to wider opportunities, lack of information about options, dilettantism, and hasty retreats into marriage and mother-hood. The common thread throughout is learned help-lessness.

It blunts our determination and makes us afraid to try. As one woman put it, "I have a lot of ideas, but I don't have the courage to pursue them." Another said, "I have thought about this idea and talked to friends about it a hundred times, but I never did anything about it." There is Lois, who wants to go to law school but can't get herself to apply. There is Sharon, an aspiring actress, who has trouble getting herself to auditions. And Jeanne, who won't submit her poetry for publication. The list goes on and on.

There is a wide river between having ideas and imple-menting them. Many of us are afraid to cross it.

Lydia is a woman who was afraid to try. Although she had done very well in pre-med courses at a top-notch col-lege, she wasn't convinced that she had enough talent to be a doctor. For several years after college, she thought about going to medical school but she didn't apply. Merely applying required a commitment. It would cost several hundred dollars and many hours of study and work. So, for a long time, Lydia did nothing.

Eventually, with the aid of therapy, she took the plunge. The application process was an ongoing battle be-tween her desire to be a doctor and her self-doubts and inclination to avoid. She struggled to get herself to fill out applications, to explain in three hundred words why she wanted to be a doctor and why medical schools should admit her. Television became an ideal way to avoid studying for the entrance exam. And, fearing she was wasting peo-ple's time, she felt hesitant to ask for recommendations. As with many other talented women, learned helplessness pro-duced doubts and fears in Lydia that weakened her moti-vation to act.

Despite all this, Lydia finally got through the application process. To her surprise and delight, her professors wrote that she was an unusually gifted student. She was even more amazed at being accepted to several top-ranking medical schools.

Lydia's success notwithstanding, even when we do try, some of us aren't persistent enough. When we encounter real obstacles, we get discouraged easily and give up too soon. One woman wrote an exceptional doctoral dissertation for which she received high praise. She wrote an article based on the thesis and submitted it to two scholarly journals. When the article was rejected by both, she dropped the matter. She lost interest in it and, in her own words, "became lazy."

Lack of persistence can show up in surprising places. An engineer in an electronics company, a seemingly unlikely victim of learned helplessness, made this discovery when she received her performance review. Her supervisor told her that she wasn't persistent enough in dealing with technical problems. He felt she could handle most of the problems she brought to him if she gave herself half a chance. The review was surprising, but fair. She admitted that most of the time she didn't have any difficulty with her work, but when she did, she gave up almost immediately and went to her boss for help.

Learned helplessness makes us vulnerable to interpreting any serious difficulty as evidence of inevitable failure. Pulling out appears to be the most reasonable course of action. After all, why beat a dead horse?

This reasoning guided the thinking of a self-employed consultant whose business was in trouble. When she lost her biggest account, her first thought was to close her doors. Instead of devoting her attention to getting new accounts, she diverted herself with reveries of that all-purpose miracle-cure: marriage. Although she had sworn off marriage after a messy divorce, she began to consider marrying her lover of five years.

Withdrawal from problem solving can be subtle. An administrative assistant, who complained about having trouble getting organized, presented an interesting problem. She could remember and organize a great many discrete tasks: typing memos, running errands, making phone calls, etc. But she had great difficulty organizing the smaller parts of one large project. For example, when writing reports, she had trouble figuring out what was important and what should go where. When confronted with this type of work, she avoided it as long as possible and sometimes never got around to it.

What was the problem? Certainly it wasn't lack of general intelligence or analytical ability. She had plenty of both. It all boiled down to persistence. She didn't look at the material long enough to gain the familiarity needed to arrange it in a reasonable order. If she couldn't organize it immediately, she concluded that she couldn't do it at all. She developed a habit of avoiding these types of projects. This made it difficult for her to develop the needed skills, and reinforced her sense of inadequacy.

Some of us have learned helplessness to such an extent that even a slight frustration or setback is enough to make us call it quits. Typically, we describe ourselves as people who don't follow through or who drop out. Our lives are full of unfinished projects: uncompleted college degrees, course work, résumés, paintings, and books.

Whether to hold or to fold when the chips are down is always a judgment call. At times discretion is the better part of valor. But those of us who habitually avoid and withdraw know who we are.

One of the deadlier effects of learned helplessness is that motivational difficulties, like viruses, can spread. Lack of initiative and persistence in one set of circumstances can carry over to a totally different situation. Does helplessness in math interfere with the ability to compete in, say, tennis? Perhaps.

Psychologists have found that helplessness in problem solving can inhibit normal competitiveness in an unrelated situation.[11] College students were divided into three groups and asked to solve either an impossible puzzle, a solvable one, or none at all. In the second half of the study, they played a game. On taking his or her turn, each player had a choice of competing, cooperating, or withdrawing. Researchers observed that the students who had been asked to solve the impossible puzzle—the uncontrollable situation—withdrew more and competed less in the game than did the other students.

While trivial experiences with circumstances beyond our control won't do much damage, serious ones can cause real harm. Getting stalled in a subway tunnel may be unsettling, but it won't make us doubt our ability to function. On the other hand, feeling defeated on the job can destroy one's initiative to improve the situation or seek a better one.

Being unhappy at work can create a sense of helplessness that carries over to the job hunt and makes it more difficult to find a new job. Nicole, for example, described a period of several days when she was unable to write cover letters to accompany her résumé when she applied for jobs. She started, found them lacking, and then quit. It turned out that in the previous week her boss had made Nicole feel like a powerless failure. He had transferred one of her subordinates to another department without notifying her. Her subordinate told her of the fait accompli. Downhearted, Nicole couldn't believe things would be better elsewhere. Struggling to write cover letters seemed pointless.

Because learned helplessness can generalize from one area to another, it can spread paralysis throughout patterns of adaptive behavior. At worst, it can undermine initiative and persistence entirely. A case in point is one woman who felt helpless about her inability to lose weight, a goal she valued above all others. Feeling helpless about her weight, she couldn't take charge of any other part of her life. She couldn't get herself to change a boring job, leave a dull lover, or move from an inconvenient, overpriced apartment.

Misplaced Attention.   Up to now we have been look-ing at overt behavior: what we do or don't do out in the world. Whether we initiate action or never get started; per-severe in the face of obstacles or quit prematurely. How-ever, learned helplessness has an impact on what goes on inside our head as well. It has enormous influence on the content of our thoughts.

In order to accomplish anything we must think about our goal and the tasks needed to achieve it. Even when not actually working on our project, we need to be thinking about it in the back of our mind. We must be focused on it. Without this focused attention our goal is difficult, if not impossible, to achieve.

Learned helplessness shifts our attention away from our goal and goal-related tasks.

Think of a goal as a target. We look at it briefly, assume we can't hit it, and then turn away. We stop thinking about it in a serious, active, creative manner and start thinking about something else. We find ourselves in the same pre-dicament as the man who, having lost his keys, looks for them under the street lamp. A stranger comes along and asks, "Is this where you lost them?" "No," the man replies, "but this is where the light is." Similarly, we shift our attention from goal-related matters to a place where we feel greater psychological comfort.

When we misplace attention at the beginning of the project, initiative is inhibited or completely destroyed. If we don't focus on our goal, if we take our eyes off the ball, our ideas are vague. And, if we aren't clear about what we want, it's hard to figure out how to get it. Sometimes the goal is clear-cut, but we get stuck because we have shifted our attention away from the means to achieve it.

When we misplace attention during the course of the project, as we encounter obstacles, persistence is undermined. This is unfortunate because most complex projects run into problems. Murphy's Law operates: Something always goes wrong. If we shift our focus away from the difficulties, our hands are tied. Whatever resources we possess—intelligence, energy, relationships, time, money—aren't brought to bear on the matter. We make it impossible to persist and solve problems.

The shift of attention may be temporary or permanent. Some dreams are defeated by learned helplessness. We turn away and never look back. But in other cases our goals are so compelling, for practical or psychological reasons, that they develop a life of their own. They won't let go of us. They seem to tug at our sleeves, saying "Don't abandon me." When this happens our attention shifts back and forth between our project and other things. We alternate, in a tension-filled way reminiscent of a tug-of-war, between focusing on our project and ignoring it.

The net result of this vacillation is that we think about our goal and tasks—but not enough. We don't give them the frequent, consistent attention required to formulate an effective plan of action. We end up with ideas that lack the coherence needed to proceed with confidence. Under these circumstances, if we take action at all, we start and stop repeatedly, limit our productivity, and usually fail to make any real progress.

This was the situation that made Harriet, an energetic twenty-eight-year-old woman who wanted to buy a home, feel stuck. Her father, a real estate attorney, conveyed the impression that buying real estate was akin to swimming with sharks, a questionable activity for an inexperienced single woman. He made offers of help, which Harriet, wishing to be independent, rejected. Unfortunately, despite her bravado, Daddy's message found its mark, and she was terrified. She couldn't focus consistently enough to create a clear picture of what she wanted. Her concept kept changing as one idea or another struck her fancy. One week she was going to buy a cottage in the country, the next a condo in the city. One day she was going to borrow money from her family, the next she was going to swing it on her own.

Harriet's house-hunting strategy was just as confused. When the mood struck, she circled ads in the newspaper. Sometimes she followed through with phone calls, other times she didn't. Every now and then she talked to realtors and some weekends she went to open houses. After many months of this type of activity Harriet had made no purchase.

Vacillation patterns can be intricate. Since most major projects consist of many elements, we may not respond to all of them with learned helplessness. We may do some tasks with enthusiasm and ignore or vacillate about others. This is a common problem among self-employed women. Some of us create fabulous jewelry, outcook restaurant chefs, or write brilliantly. We pay a great deal of attention to our craft. But the business aspects of the work feel intimidating and we don't pay enough attention to them. When it comes to focusing on marketing and finance, to expanding the business from a marginally profitable "hobby" to a money-making enterprise, our eyes glaze over. Our minds wander. The fog rolls in. We pay just enough attention to maintain a hand-to-mouth existence, but not enough to make serious money. And we wonder, our families wonder, our friends wonder, our clients wonder: With all that talent, why aren't we making it big?

One reason misplaced attention is so troublesome is that we don't know we have misplaced it. We fail to notice that we have changed our position, are no longer facing the target, and can't possibly hit the bull's-eye. Mistakenly, we imagine we should be hitting our mark.

We are miserable, not only due to our inaction but because we are confused. We are motivated, yet some unknown force keeps us from our mission. It makes no sense. It never occurs to us that an unrecognized shift of attention is a major cause of being stuck.

Unable to grasp the nature of the problem, we struggle to fill the gap in our understanding. Once again we look in the wrong places and fill that gap with imagined—and real, albeit irrelevant—inadequacies. We blame our lack of self-esteem, intelligence, skill, confidence, talent.

Let's look at Eileen, for example. A lawyer who actively disliked her job, she was trying to account for why she hadn't resigned. She compared herself unfavorably to a real estate developer friend who was doing condo conversions. Noting her friend's penchant for living on the edge, Eileen explained, "My problem must be that I am not a risk-taker." Not really. Her problem was that she hadn't given enough attention to what she wanted to do next. Unclear about her future direction, Eileen was disinclined to make any move. Making major changes without inner clarity made her feel as if she were jumping into a black hole. Small wonder she wasn't ready to resign.

Misplacing attention is like having a loose wire in the car. It may be a small problem that is easily repaired. But, if we don't spot it and fix it, we aren't going anywhere.

Disrupted Learning

Imagine trying to learn to play the piano and not being able to tell the right notes from the wrong ones. It would be impossible. In order to learn, we have to be able to tell the difference between the good moves and the bad ones. If we can't recognize the good moves, we have trouble learning.

Recall how Dr. Seligman's old dogs sat passively while being subjected to shocks. Occasionally, a few of them, after receiving several shocks, jumped over the barrier and escaped their discomfort.[12] But unlike the new dogs, who kept right on jumping and escaping the shocks, the old dogs didn't do it again. Instead, they reverted to their original passive state and continued to get shocked. They didn't make the connection between jumping over the barrier and avoiding the pain. Convinced they were helpless, they failed to notice they had done something right, and it didn't occur to them to repeat it. Because they didn't perceive their success, they couldn't learn from it.

Research tells us that certain children have the same problem. In the course of studying intellectual achievement, psychologists looked at how both helpless and mastery-oriented (those with a sense of optimism about their ability to control their environment) children responded to success. Dr. Carol Deiner and Dr. Carol Dweck gave a group of ten-year-olds a set of puzzles to solve and arranged it so that all the children would have a series of successes.[13] At the end, they asked the children to judge their performance. The results were revealing.

The mastery-oriented children remembered their successes and accurately recalled how many problems they had solved correctly. When asked to compare themselves with other children, they thought they had done better than their peers. Seeing their current success as an indicator of ability, they anticipated success in the future.

The helpless children, on the other hand, didn't seem to see themselves as having been successful. They underestimated the number of problems they had solved correctly. When comparing themselves to their peers, they assumed others had done better. This was the case even when they had gotten every problem right. Not surprisingly, they didn't think their current performance gave them reason to have high expectations for the future.

Why did the helpless dogs and children have difficulty perceiving success? The answer lies in the idea of *unlearning*. Imagine a friend, Jane Smith, who gets married and changes her name to Jane Jones. For a long time afterward we tend to think of her as Jane Smith. A link between a particular person and the name Smith has been forged in our mind. It's difficult to undo that connection and think Jones. Jane's new acquaintances, however, like the new dogs and the mastery-oriented children, don't have a problem since they have nothing to unlearn.

Uncontrollable situations teach us that there is no causal relationship between what we do and what happens in a particular set of circumstances. Our actions don't matter because they have no impact on events. Outcomes, negative or positive, have no connection with our activities. Good results aren't indicators of personal effectiveness any more than a sunny day would be.

Once we acquire the mental set that our actions are irrelevant, it's hard to shift gears. It's difficult to unlearn learned helplessness and to believe that we can have impact. When we are successful, we don't make the connection between our efforts and the favorable outcome. We don't get the fact that we made it happen. We don't perceive our success.

Celia, a woman in middle management in a large computer company, thought she was a failure in her work. The only woman at her managerial level, she felt isolated and unappreciated. In fact, *she* was overlooking her successes on the job. To begin with, she was the first woman to achieve her rank. Second, she had been promoted rapidly. Third, when she spoke up, she was heard; when she exercised authority, she got results. And finally, during a hiring freeze, she had been permitted to hire additional personnel. The person guilty of depriving Celia of appreciation was Celia herself.

The feminine discounting habit is both a cause and an effect of the inability to perceive success. Learning rules of causality that discount our actions and abilities is one way of learning that our actions are inconsequential. Once ingrained, the discounting habit perpetuates feelings of helplessness. Instead of focusing on the connections between our behavior and good results, we ignore and deny them. We believe positive outcomes have nothing to do with us. A consultant who saved a company hundreds of thousands of dollars accounted for it by saying, "I was lucky. I got the right information quickly." Lucky? Surely she jests. But no, she was serious. This highly intelligent and accomplished woman failed to make the connection between her actions and the successful outcome. She was able to size up the situation quickly and accurately, to ask for the right information, and to request it in a manner that made people take her seriously and bring it to her posthaste. And once she got the information she was able to use it expertly. Intellectually and interpersonally she performed beautifully and she didn't know it.

In order to perceive success, many of us have to unlearn—in gut reactions as well as in our minds—old messages about women's abilities, roles, and limitations. These old tapes make us oblivious to our successes in the same way the helpless dogs were oblivious to the fact that they had found the way to escape the shocks.

Emotional Distress

When uncontrollable events are traumatic or unpleasant, they can create feelings of anxiety and depression. Research tells us that both animals and people respond to helplessness with physical symptoms we all recognize as stress. White laboratory rats subjected to uncontrollable shocks were far more nervous than rats who could escape them by pressing a knob.[14] The helpless rats ate and drank less, defecated more often, and had more ulcers.

In an analogous study, people were subjected to shocks while working on puzzles.[15] One group could stop the shocks whenever they wished, while a second group had no control. Blood pressure, measured every thirty seconds, was consistently higher for the helpless group. For those who have learned helplessness, anxiety is the emotional response to uncertainty.[16]

This hits home for women struggling to achieve. Anxiety, fear, apprehension, lack of confidence: These are our experiences as we approach various aspects of our work. Since traditional femininity has taught us that we lack ability and the power to control, we venture forth uncertainly, particularly in nontraditional realms. We are plagued not only with feelings of personal inadequacy but with the suspicion that—as women—we know less about the ways of the world than do our male counterparts. This adds to our tension.

Some of us feel anxious every time we approach major—and even not-so-major—challenges. The uncertainty stirs up feelings of learned helplessness. We might be facing an uncontrollable situation. It seems too close to call: possible or impossible? We won't know until all the votes are in. In the meantime, half of our mind is convinced that the mission is impossible. As one panicked woman put it, "I can't do it. I don't want to do it. Help, get me out of here!"

Chris, a business manager in a nonprofit organization, was faced with a government audit. She had to prepare a complicated financial report and, being new at that job, she couldn't make sense of some figures from the previous year. She looked at the numbers briefly, couldn't figure them out immediately, and had a massive anxiety attack. She sat and stared at the papers. Her mind went totally blank. Although she was a highly experienced accountant, for most of that day she couldn't retrieve the competent part of herself.

Fortunately, these feelings tend to have a time limit and go away eventually. But while we are living through them, we suffer and we waste time and energy. For some of us, this has become a ritual that we engage in, perhaps to appease the gods for the sin of pride, before we set about to cope.

In some cases, this ritual is performed regularly on a smaller scale when we face the problem of getting started. We have difficulty writing the first sentences, solving the first problems, reading the first pages. We give new meaning to the word "procrastination." The contortions are endless. Once past the initial hurdle, we can enjoy the work and do it well. Often we feel relief and even elation and wonder why we fussed so much. Yet powerful feelings of learned helplessness force us to go through this ritual time and time again.

Anxiety disappears once it becomes apparent that the situation is controllable. On the other hand, if we believe that nothing can be done, according to Seligman, depression results.[17] Clinical work with women who feel stuck bears this out. When those of us who have learned helplessness don't achieve immediate success, we interpret this lack of immediate success as validation of our assumption of helplessness. We conclude that we will never succeed, and we get discouraged and depressed. This makes it difficult for us to bounce back and try again. Failure to persist increases our sense of helplessness and perpetuates feelings of depression. We are caught in a vicious cycle and we feel stuck.

THE CURE

Learned helplessness isn't a terminal ailment. It can be cured.

Dr. Seligman cured his dogs by actually hauling them over the barrier until they figured out that jumping over it would allow them to escape the shocks.[18] It took being tossed over the fence anywhere from twenty-five to two hundred times before the dogs got the idea. At first they were like deadweights. But as the training progressed, less and less force was needed to move the dogs. Eventually, the dogs initiated their own responses.

This is similar to what happens to those of us who have learned helplessness. At first we have resistance to being jarred out of our lethargy. Calls for action are oppressive, unrealistic, meaningless noises: well intentioned but irritating. But once we start to do battle with helplessness and discover that our efforts bring results, we begin to feel differently. Once we view action positively, our helplessness declines.

How do we get there? Well, obviously we can't get people to haul us over barriers. Instead, we have to haul ourselves, with a little help from our friends. We must begin to act, to focus on our actions, and to observe the consequences. In this way, we can learn to connect actions with outcome and to recognize success when we have it. Specific strategies and techniques for doing this will be discussed in Part II. But first, let's look at the flip side of learned helplessness: the mastery orientation.

CHAPTER 3

Action

*H*arry Hatfield is a modern American success story. Born and raised in a working-class neighborhood in Boston, he began life modestly. Now he is a millionaire.

Harry graduated from the local state college with average grades as a physics major. This convinced him he wasn't cut out to be a physicist. Instead, he took a job with a leading national electronics company. He went around the country selling what I will call (for the sake of confidentiality) "widgets." His gregariousness made him popular with his customers and his sales mounted. But he wasn't content to be a successful salesman; he wanted something more, so he kept his eyes open.

He noticed there was a hole in the market, a need to be filled. Companies needed more individualized attention to their particular problems. They needed consultants as well as salespeople to help them choose and use widgets more effectively.

This type of service wasn't profitable for the big widget manufacturers. Their sales staffs didn't have time to sit down with a company and get a detailed picture of its operation. They simply went in and offered their product.

Harry set up an office in his basement, ordered business cards, and became a consultant. When his business grew large enough to be self-sustaining, he quit his sales job and began making and selling his own widgets. He moved out of his basement and into a small plant.

Then the economy began to get rocky. While the interest rates on his loans were soaring, his sales were declining. These were difficult conditions for a young business, but Harry didn't pack up his widgets and go home. He maintained his faith. As he put it, "Times are rough. So we just have to work harder. We have to advertise more and put more effort into getting new business."

This Horatio Alger story illustrates a frame of mind more characteristic of men than of women: the mastery orientation. The mastery orientation is a sense of optimism about one's ability to control events. It's the sum total of a cluster of attitudes toward ourselves and our work that allows us to take action and to strive for achievement.

It's useful to think of it as being made up of three interrelated parts: (1) a set of values, (2) a perception of control, and (3) a positive reaction to challenge.

The mastery orientation places a high premium on both the ends and the means. It values actual products—Nobel prizes, Olympic medals, Academy Awards, self-made riches—but more important than any particular success is the process that created it. Taking action, setting goals and working toward them deliberately and effectively, is an end in itself. The striving, the struggling, and the persevering are what count.

Action is glorified in Horatio Alger stories, tales of adventure, political speeches, and job classifieds. Wanted: ambitious, resourceful person who likes challenge. The hero thinks big, aims high, and takes risks. He is undaunted by adversity. Obstacles are there to be overcome. When the going gets tough, the tough get going.

The expectation that one can exert influence on one's environment is at the heart of the mastery orientation. Believing this allows us to act, to take initiative, assume responsibility, and make commitments. With it comes the persistence to solve problems and the ability to perceive success and maintain a sense of optimism about future accomplishments.

The perception of control doesn't guarantee success, but it does give us the feeling that we have a fighting chance.

When we combine values that stress action with a perception of control, the result is a positive attitude toward challenge. Both ingredients are necessary. Values that encourage striving, whatever the outcome, allow us to respect our efforts. We increase our self-esteem simply by trying. But values aren't enough. Without a perception of control, we feel helpless and see no reason to try. On the other hand, if a situation looks controllable, we can tackle it with gusto, propelled by the desire to succeed and the respect for persistence.

With a positive attitude, we see problems as challenges and approach them with curiosity. We don't immediately interpret difficulty as defeat. Just because one road is closed, it doesn't mean the entire trip must be canceled. If one tactic doesn't work, another will. We just have to keep trying until we hit upon the solution.

Not only does a positive attitude toward challenge permit us to cope with difficulties as they arise, it allows us to anticipate problems in advance. Unafraid, we plan for trouble. A carpenter expressed this idea beautifully. I asked him how long it would take to install kitchen cabinets. He replied, "It takes two days to install them, and a third day to handle the screw-ups that always come along."

THE INHIBITED MASTERY ORIENTATION

Somewhere between a sense of optimism about one's ability to control events and learned helplessness is a middle ground that I call the inhibited mastery orientation. Here, instead of seeing "possible" or "impossible," we see "limited possibilities."

Traditionally, many forces have operated to inhibit women's mastery orientation and, despite social changes, they still exert an impact on our lives. One important force is the way we rear and educate children. Socialization practices both deliberately and inadvertently subvert women's sense of optimism by: (1) de-emphasizing mastery-oriented values, (2) undermining girls' perception of control, (3) giving girls insufficient encouragement to confront challenge, (4) restricting freedom to explore the environment, and (5) giving mixed messages.

Values

In the land of sex role stereotypes, power, action, and challenge are part of the male domain. This is most apparent in the extreme concept of *machismo*. The macho man can handle anything and everything. He believes he is always in control. Facing unbeatable odds, he knows no fear, no retreat. He fights to the finish, snatching victory from the jaws of defeat.

While men act, women attract. If conquering the world

is man's mission, loving is woman's. Women were traditionally expected to find fulfillment in the emotional ties of
relationships. Action and achievement were considered foreign to women's basic nature, unfeminine. Women were
urged and forced to be dependent on men, to restrict their
sphere to home and hearth. Consequently, women had less
opportunity to adopt the values of the mastery orientation.

Cultural change notwithstanding, traditional expectations remain strong. Society still doesn't value or encourage
action and achievement in women as it does in men. One
bright twenty-six-year-old woman described her experience:
"No one demanded anything of me as I was growing up.
Just smile and Daddy will take care of everything. All I had
to do was be there and be nice. The only thing was that I
had to do well in school. But that really wasn't achievement.
It was being a good girl, not embarrassing my parents by
doing badly. From the outside, it gave people a sense that
I was achieving, but really it was doing nothing. The road
was totally paved."

Several research studies, including a large-scale national survey, found that parents expect more achievement,
self-reliance, independence, and responsibility from their
sons than from their daughters.[1] On the other hand, parents
expect their daughters to be more attractive, kind, well-
mannered, unselfish, and to have a good marriage and good
children.

Expectations get translated into actions. Adults, particularly men, are more encouraging of mastery-oriented behavior in boys than in girls. In one study, researchers
watched parents teach their children.[2] Boys' fathers were
concerned about their sons learning the tasks. They set high
standards, paid attention to the cognitive elements of the
tasks, and stressed achievement. In contrast, the fathers of
girls paid less attention to the tasks and spent more time
playing, joking, encouraging, and protecting.

Another study had an intriguing twist, mildly reminiscent of a Shakespearean comedy.[3] A two-year-old child was dressed up as a boy in one half of the study and as a girl in the other half. As we would by now expect, the adults, particularly the men, expected the "boy" to do better than the "girl," and they rewarded the "boy" more for trying to achieve goals than they did the "girl."

Our educational system, the guardian of talent and intellect, also appears to de-emphasize the mastery orientation in girls. Teachers view girls and boys differently.[4] In one study, when teachers evaluated boys, they stressed performance and work habits. When they evaluated girls, they emphasized friendly, agreeable behavior. Since this was a school situation, not a social tea, we would expect the emphasis to be on academic ability for all children. Apparently not. Furthermore, while the teachers could tell the bright boys from the average ones, they didn't discriminate between bright and average girls.

After reviewing the research, Dr. Jeanne Block, a psychologist at the University of California at Berkeley and a noted authority on the development of sex differences in personality, concluded that girls' intellectual achievement is passively ignored and often even actively discouraged at all educational levels, from nursery school through college.[5]

Children's books and television programs sing the same song.[6] Boys act, girls watch. Boys invent, girls use the inventions. Boys rescue, girls get rescued. Boys use ingenuity to solve problems, girls burst into tears and run to others for help. Boys are rewarded for action, girls can be punished for being too active. The lyrics change, but the tune remains the same.

We all learn from what we are explicitly taught and from what we observe around us. If we are encouraged to set a wide variety of goals and to work toward them, we are likely to value action. If we are encouraged to strive for excellence in our activities, we are likely to value achievement. Women have the opportunity to acquire the values of the mastery orientation only to the extent that they have the opportunity to learn these lessons.

Perception of Control

Anyone who has ever seen a group of teenaged boys strut down Main Street or saunter through a subway car has seen a perception of control. These young men know that their presence has an impact; they do not go unnoticed.

Males, more than females, assume that they can influence their environment, that the world is responsive to their actions.[7] Feelings of potency and effectiveness are an important part of their self-images. Males describe themselves as being more energetic, powerful, ambitious, and able to control external events than do their female counterparts.

How does this state of affairs come about? Obviously, men have most of the political and economic power. But how does that reality become embedded in our perceptions in matters that have no direct bearing on issues of male dominance? The answer can be found in understanding how the perception of control is acquired. Basically, we can learn it in two ways: We can experience control directly or we can be told that we have it.

When we press an elevator button and the elevator arrives, we get immediate feedback that our action has been effective.

We have a direct experience of control when we receive what psychologists call *contingent responses*: specific cause-and-effect reactions to our initiatives. We press a button and an elevator arrives. We give people hugs and they hug us back. Or we give people punches and they punch us back. In each case, there is a clear connection between what we dish out and what we get back.

We all need contingent responses throughout our lives. But they are particularly important to the developing child.[8] Much of childhood activity is devoted to discovering how the world reacts to our overtures. What happens when we take apart the alarm clock? What happens when we kick baby sister in the shins?

If the world is full of elevators that arrive after children press the buttons, they will be impressed with their ability to make things happen. On the other hand, if nothing happens when children press buttons, they will be less convinced of their ability to exert control. The more contingent responses children receive, the more likely they are to develop a perception of control.

In reviewing research on socialization practices, Dr. Block found that girls get fewer contingent responses, in the form of attention, responsiveness, encouragement, and criticism, than do boys.[9]

Differences begin in early infancy. In one study, researchers observed mothers while they fed their babies.[10] They found that boys' mothers were more attentive to their infants' signals than were girls' mothers. These types of differences continue throughout childhood. Fathers in particular seem to give more feedback to their sons than to their daughters. Whether the feedback is positive, such as approval, talk, and physical affection, or negative, such as disapproval, corporal punishment, and yelling, girls seem to get less of it.[11]

Teachers are also less likely to respond to girls' initiatives.[12] When a student wasn't called on in class, the student was more likely to be a girl. When pupils raised their hands with questions, teachers less often responded to girls. When they did respond, they were less helpful, giving girls less specific information. Teachers even recognized and rewarded creativity less frequently in girls than in boys.

Toys, too, differ in the amount of responsiveness they offer children. Boys get a greater variety of interesting toys that encourage manipulation and innovation.[13] Compare an erector set with a doll. There's nothing wrong with dolls, but, like most girls' toys, they don't offer much opportunity for inventiveness and they encourage imitation.

After surveying a host of studies, Dr. Block concluded that boys benefit from the greater number of contingent responses given them.[14] These benefits include increased motivation and goal orientation, and an awareness of their ability to elicit reactions from their environment. Boys are more likely than girls to develop assumptions about themselves and their world that enable them to perceive control.

We don't actually have to press an elevator button to know we can command the elevator. We can learn that from any credible authority. This bit of information becomes part of our collection of knowledge and our perception of control.

A fascinating study demonstrates the powerful effects of what we are told. Researchers studying stress in the urban environment attempted to re-create the stress by simulating city noises.[15] They asked three groups of college students to complete some tasks while being subjected to a cacophony of loud, incongruous sounds: one person speaking Armenian, two people speaking Spanish, a typewriter, a mimeograph machine, a calculator.

One group of students was able to turn off the noise when they wished and they performed well. The second group, which could not turn off the noise, did poorly on the tasks. They were less persistent in solving problems, did badly on proofreading, and were irritated.

The third group provided the really interesting twist. They were deliberately misled. They were told that they could stop the noise by pressing a button (in fact they couldn't), but they were requested not to do so. Despite the unrelenting noise, these students functioned as well as those who turned off the blare.

"True it is if you think it is," observed the playwright Pirandello. The third group of students behaved as if they had control. Because they were given the perception of control, even though it was unfounded, they were able to avoid the debilitating effects of helplessness.

We are taught the perception of control by can-do messages. They convey that a particular action is both realistically possible and socially acceptable. These messages can come in the form of direct statements: "Yes, you can go around the block by yourself." "Sure, it's possible for a good swimmer to make it across the lake." "When you grow up, you can run for mayor." "If at first you don't succeed, try again."

Role models also provide can-do messages. Astronauts demonstrate that it's possible to land on the moon. Working mothers show that women can have competence outside of the home. The more plentiful the role models and the wider their range of activity and power, the more positive messages we get. Conversely, the fewer the role models and the more limited their range of activity and power, the fewer positive messages we get.

Teaching conveys the can-do messages that it is both possible and acceptable for us to learn. This is why teachers, mentors, and coaches are so critical to the development of skill and talent. By giving both permission and tools for mastery, they aid enormously in developing the perception of control.

When you come right down to it, a good deal of bringing up children is simply a matter of teaching them what they can and can't do.

Unfortunately, girls have gotten too many can't-do and too few can-do messages. Traditional role models have been limited in number, range of behavior, and power. Access to learning and training has been restricted. Although our feet haven't been bound in the ancient Chinese tradition, much of what has been deemed appropriate feminine behavior has consisted of *not* doing. A lady mustn't fight, can't understand math or fly a jet, shouldn't run for president. While some of this has changed, negative doctrines continue to make their impact.

Freedom

The French writer Simone de Beauvoir once made the provocative suggestion that adolescent girls are so dependent on male companionship because their lives are so confined and dull that they can't give each other enough stimulation. They need boys to bring them the excitement of the wider world.[16]

While research doesn't report on "dullness," it does present a consistent picture of girls having less freedom to explore their environment than boys.[17] Girls' activities are more restricted and closely supervised. They are encouraged to stay in or near their home. When chores are divided up, they are more likely to be given chores in the house, while boys get the ones outside or away from it. Girls are expected to run errands at a later age than boys (although they aren't held back from housebound tasks such as putting away clothes) and are allowed fewer independent trips away from home. Girls are usually not allowed to roam a wide range of the community without getting permission.

These research results are hardly front-page news. They confirm what we all have known for years: Girls are held on a shorter leash. The reins are particularly likely to be pulled in at adolescence. Even girls who enjoyed considerable freedom during childhood find that their formerly liberal parents become increasingly curious about and restrictive of their activities. At a time when life is opening up for males, it's constricting for many females.

Homebound messages limit horizons. If girls don't get around, they have less of a chance of seeing how the world operates. They have less opportunity to acquire and practice a broad range of skills, to solve problems, and to gain self-knowledge.

Excessive restrictions convey the message that the wider world is too difficult or dangerous for girls to handle and implicitly encourage avoidance as a way of coping.

These messages create anxiety, which can be seen in adult women who fear traveling alone. In its more extreme form, this anxiety can be seen in agoraphobia (predominantly a woman's problem), where women are unable to leave their homes by themselves.

Challenge

Would you rather work on a puzzle you have already solved or one you have failed to solve?

Several studies have found that when children were given the choice of pursuing a difficult problem or escaping it, boys were more likely to choose the challenge, while girls tended to pick an easy success or to leave the scene.[18]

Acquiring a positive attitude toward challenge, something that girls seem to do less than boys, involves being exposed to obstacles, confronting them, and persisting long enough to have a chance to overcome them.

In a variety of ways, girls have less exposure to a wide range of challenges. As we have already seen, girls get around less and have less opportunity to run into novel situations. In the classroom, as well, during the elementary school years, work is generally easier for girls than for boys. And in the subjects where girls often have difficulty, such as math and science, they may be excused from challenge on the ground that they lack innate aptitude.

Teachers are less likely to tell girls to try harder, partially because teachers give girls less attention to begin with, and partially because teachers tend to assume that girls are doing their best. One study found that teachers attributed boys' work failures to lack of motivation eight times more often than girls'.[19] Being told to try harder is being told that one has ability and should persist.

Bright girls, in particular, are likely to suffer from this type of neglect. When they are doing adequate work, others often don't notice that they are underachieving. One very bright young woman, currently struggling with underachievement problems, described her elementary school years in an affluent suburb: "I didn't have to do anything until the seventh grade. Then, when real demands were placed on me, I got very upset." I have many clients like this who weren't encouraged to stretch themselves and missed too many opportunities to confront and master problems.

Excessive help, too much or too soon, is another way girls are discouraged. Research has found that mothers are more solicitous of girls than of boys.[20] After a frustrating experience, mothers gave hugs and other types of physical comfort more immediately to girls than to boys. In situations where children were attempting to solve problems, mothers were more responsive to bids for help from girls than from boys. While boys' mothers ignored or denied requests for aid a good deal of the time, girls' mothers consistently gave help and encouragement—even when it wasn't needed.

Women who have gotten stuck often describe childhoods filled with too much help. Daddy coming to the rescue with the science project was a particularly memorable event. Instead of offering *some* help while demanding that their daughters solve their own problems, these fathers did the entire project themselves. This type of scenario is good for a few laughs in a television sitcom, but it has serious consequences in real life.

Overprotecting girls undercuts their ability to take difficulty in stride and to solve problems. It undermines the perception of control, a positive attitude toward challenge, self-reliance, and it encourages the development of avoidance tactics instead of coping strategies.

All this gets compounded when passivity is linked with feminine allure. As one young woman said recently, "Struggling isn't attractive. A female is much more appealing if she isn't working at things, if she is just bubbleheaded and spontaneous. It's not okay to be dumb, but it's okay to be helpless—that gets you things."

The damsel in distress cliché glamorizes helplessness.

It's terribly romantic to be rescued by a knight in shining armor. For example, in the movie *Raiders of the Lost Ark*, even a presumably liberated heroine who fights and drinks men under the table is destined to be rescued by the swashbuckling Indiana Jones. The moral of the story is as old as the hills: To solve our problems, all we really need to do is *wait* for a man.

When we don't get rescued, we must endure: Wait, and this too shall pass. While men are encouraged to tolerate discomfort in the pursuit of a goal, women have been encouraged simply to endure. Many women are remarkable in their ability to accept, tolerate, put up with, or make the best of rotten situations. Often this takes strength and has survival value in times where options are very limited. It has probably gotten millions through wars, famines, and disease. But in times of opportunity or social change, stoic forbearance can interfere with active problem solving.

Values that glorify passivity in the name of womanhood subvert a positive attitude toward challenge and encourage excessive dependency on others.

Mixed Messages

A high school senior sent a letter to *Ms.* magazine in which she wrote, "My girl friends want to become doctors and lawyers and such, but I still hear things like . . . 'You have to play dumb to get a boy' and 'I'm not good in math because I am a girl.' "[21]

This is the crux of a major problem: confusing, contradictory messages that say do and don't in the same breath. Be sharp, but not too sharp. Achieve, but feel free to let yourself off the hook when confronted with serious challenge. Aspire, but never forget you are a woman. Translation: Don't expect to get too far.

The do's and don'ts come in all sizes and shapes: Do well in school, but come straight home afterward because it isn't safe for you to be on your own. Or, you can do anything you want, but go to college; you need an education in case your husband dies. Each woman gets her own unique assortment. The types of messages, their timing, intensity, and consistency, all affect the ultimate package.

One woman's assortment consisted of a series of red and green lights as she was growing up. When she was a child, achievement was important to her parents and she won their approval by playing the piano extremely well. Once she reached adolescence it all changed. Academic achievement took second place to social success. Her father in particular wanted her to be the belle of the ball at the country club. He wanted her to dress like and socialize with the children of his affluent friends. Fitting into Father's conception of the female role became top priority. By the time she finished college, the lights turned green once more as her parents pushed professional achievement by urging her to go to law school.

Women who receive both very intense and consistent do and don't messages are the most likely to get stuck and to feel miserable about it. Typically these women come from backgrounds where achievement was highly valued in the abstract, but where their perception of control was under-mined in daily life. On the one hand, they were told they had talent and were encouraged, or even pressured, to become successful. On the other hand, in day-to-day living, they were discouraged from gaining the psychological in-dependence that those achievements require.

One extremely gifted woman was told that the sky was the limit. She was taught to ski, play tennis, ride horses, paint, and play the violin. She was always told that she could be the best at whatever she chose. But at the same time she was never permitted to make an independent decision. Every waking minute of every day was planned out for her. What she did, how she behaved, what she wore, what she ate, who her friends were—her life was totally controlled and regimented.

Women like this are put into a double bind: "Be an astronaut, fly to the moon, but don't go around the block by yourself." Often the achievement is far off in the distant future while the day-to-day reality is confining.

The women with the most severe problems often come from homes where parents actively undermined their daughters' independence. In one breath these parents would pressure their daughters to achieve, and in the next they would demand that their daughters remain dependent. One brilliant woman was urged to become a scientist while being simultaneously told that she was incompetent to handle her own finances. Several parents went so far as to suggest that their daughters were so incapable of taking care of themselves that prostitution might be the only means of support available to them.

It's one thing to be taught to admire success and to wish to attain it. It's quite another to be taught the independence and attitudes that make success possible. The plight of some women is that their hearts are willing but their hands feel tied.

One of the consequences of receiving powerful mixed messages is a self-image full of contradictions.

If you ask someone her height, you hardly expect her to reply, "Well, some days I am tall and some days I am short." That's a scene from *Alice in Wonderland*. Nevertheless, that's exactly how some of us, often very intelligent and talented women, evaluate our abilities. In one half of the mirror we see ourselves as competent, talented, and bound for glory. In the other half, we see ourselves as fuzzy-headed, inadequate, and just bound. Women describe these feelings in different ways. One woman said, "I see myself on the top of the heap and on the bottom simultaneously." Another remarked, "At the same time that I have great faith in my abilities, I worry that my fears of inadequacy might be true." A third, commenting on her chances of success in graduate school, said, "I *know* I can do it but I don't *think* I can." These types of images are particularly common among women who get stuck.

The split self-image isn't always apparent to either ourselves or to others. Some of us act and feel like we have the world by the tail. But upon closer inspection, the negative half of the image can be detected in the relatively limited goals we set for ourselves and the speed at which our confidence evaporates when we feel blown out of the water.

Others of us are painfully aware of our feelings of inadequacy, yet our actions belie a totally negative self-image. Despite our doubts and fears, we march forth to graduate school and to the business world and achieve considerable success. We wouldn't be able to do this if the positive side of our self-image didn't exist.

IMPACT

Girls' experiences while growing up contribute to achievement problems in adulthood. The inhibited mastery orientation creates vulnerabilities that breed difficulties with such things as responsibility, commitment, decision making, long-range planning, and stress management.

Responsibility

Women who feel stuck often describe themselves as being afraid of responsibility. They want to move forward while at the same time they distrust their ability to assume a higher level of responsibility. What makes the situation even more difficult is that they view their fear as a personal shortcoming and blame themselves for it.

The self-condemnation isn't altogether surprising. The term "responsibility" has become a popular buzzword, full of meaning, rich with moral implications. It's good to be responsible, bad to be irresponsible, and immature to avoid responsibility. Right-thinking people take responsibility for their behavior and their lives.

However, moralistic judgments neither clarify the problem nor suggest a solution. Recognizing the culprit as inhibited mastery orientation is far more productive.

Stripped of value judgments, taking responsibility is saying, to ourselves and to the world, that we will act and take the consequences of our actions. This means being able to accept the role of a doer, a primary moving force behind an event. Accepting this role when we lack a sense of optimism about our ability to influence events is a disconcerting contradiction. It simply doesn't make sense to assume responsibility voluntarily when we aren't sure we have a reasonable chance of controlling the outcome.

Commitment

One businesswoman would think about giving up her somewhat marginal public relations business every time she lost an account. For years she neither closed her shop nor made an unqualified commitment to keep it going. Unable to fish or cut bait, she dangled in limbo, feeling miserable much of the time.

Some of us get stuck in our work because we can neither make a wholehearted commitment to it nor leave it altogether. When our ship hits a reef, we don't abandon it, but neither do we determine to go down with it. We withdraw some of our emotional investment and waste time and energy on debilitating doubts. This partial withdrawal doesn't help to solve problems and creates additional tension that further undermines our already weak sense of control.

It makes sense to make commitments only when we can trust ourselves to hang in when the going gets rough. Without a positive attitude toward challenge commitments don't mean much.

Decision Making

An administrator ponders whether to cut salaries or lay off some workers. An advertising copywriter balances the pros and cons of leaving her current job to start her own agency. Everyone wants to make the right choice. Each year thousands of dollars are spent on books and seminars that teach the secrets of sound decision making.

The emphasis on technique, while necessary and useful, sometimes misses the mark. For those women who have chronic headaches with decision making, choosing between apples and oranges isn't really the issue. Underneath, we are struggling with a far more basic concern. We are confused and conflicted about our right to make decisions to begin with. Are we really entitled to think for ourselves and to act on our ideas? As one woman put it, "I keep asking myself, who am *I* to make such important decisions?"

Our private doubts create increased internal pressure to make the right choices. It's almost as if, with each major decision, our right to decide is on trial. If we don't make the correct choice, we forfeit the right to choose. While men may agonize over specific decisions, we agonize over the right to decide.

These concerns are the logical outgrowth of an inhibited mastery orientation. Decision making is the cognitive aspect of action. Or, to put it another way, action consists of a series of implemented decisions. To the extent that traditional female upbringing has stressed obedience and conformity while discouraging action, it has held back the development of skill and confidence in decision making.

Planning

"I have never set a real goal in my life," remarked one woman. She is not alone. Setting long-range goals, particularly career goals, is a foreign idea to many women. With remarkable regularity, women describe themselves as having fallen into their careers. Not only that; after having landed somewhere, they discover the concept of career goals fairly late in the game. Business consultants Dr. Margaret Hennig and Dr. Anne Jardim interviewed women managers and found that it typically took women ten years of working in their fields before advancement over the long term became a conscious goal.[22]

All this makes perfect sense when we consider that long-term planning wasn't valued in the traditional scheme of things. Our goals were preordained: marriage and children. The means of obtaining them—nonspecific, to say the least—were a mockery of the concept of planning. The best we could do was to try to be appealing and to position ourselves where a prince might find us.

So, at adolescence, when the boys were starting to think seriously about making their way in the world, many of us were choosing the perfect shade of eye shadow. Even some of us who planned to go to professional school didn't really have goals. The planning went as far as getting a degree and after that it was catch as catch can. Although much has changed, many young girls are still fuzzier and less realistic about future plans than their male counterparts.

The concept of long-range planning must be learned and practiced. It can be learned only by people who have broad horizons, who value action and achievement, and who have a great deal of faith in their ability to control their futures and to cope with the monkey wrenches that inevitably get thrown into the best-laid plans.

Stress Management

A gifted woman with a history of underachievement confessed, "My anxiety isn't all that intense, but I have a long-standing habit of avoiding it immediately."

To the extent that girls are permitted and encouraged to retreat from challenge and don't acquire mastery-oriented attitudes, they learn that difficulty and the accompanying stress are signals to withdraw. Often they find that it's acceptable to escape and avoid anxiety-producing situations. Unlike most boys, who are pressured to confront and master fear, girls are frequently allowed to feel justified in letting themselves off the hook. Girls who learn to use avoidance as a major stress-management strategy have less motivation and less opportunity to face stressful situations and to find more effective ways of handling anxiety.

When taking action becomes anxiety provoking—as it often does—those who deal with stress by avoiding it find themselves in what psychologists call an *approach-avoidance conflict*. Sometimes this expresses itself in inefficiency or in phobic reactions to specific work-related tasks such as public speaking, studying, or job hunting. At other times, the conflict expresses itself in a general sense of feeling stuck.

The good news is that while our mastery orientation may be inhibited, it hasn't been annihilated. Most of us feel optimistic about our ability to influence events in some aspects of our lives. In certain realms of endeavor, we feel eager to act, perceive control, and respond positively to challenge. In particular, women who have a track record of some accomplishment are likely to be mastery oriented in many areas.

We don't have to start our gardens from seed. We only need to actively nurture our roses. Our mission, should we accept it, is to expand our mastery orientation to more and more situations until it changes from a response to specific types of situations to a more general attitude toward all action.

CHAPTER 4

Fear of Failure

F ailure! An unpleasant word. Bad news for our self-esteem and our life. Something nobody wants. Nevertheless, failure is part and parcel of achievement. If we shield ourselves from the risk of failure by playing it safe and avoiding serious challenge, we limit our accomplishment. Achievement thrives on challenge, inherent in which is the possibility of failure.

Fear of failure comes in various guises. Some people say that they are afraid of being evaluated. But what they really fear is being judged and found lacking; no one who expects to walk off with the blue ribbon is afraid of being judged. Some people confuse fear of failure with fear of success. When we fear immediate success because we are afraid of demands for continued achievement, that's fear of failure projected into the future. We think we can jump the first hurdle but we have doubts about the subsequent hurdles—that's fear of failure. In other cases, people don't acknowledge their anxiety but do recognize the symptoms when they have difficulty assuming responsibility, making commitments, taking risks, making decisions, as well as in an assortment of work phobias.

Females appear to experience more fear of failure than do males. In numerous studies, children were given questionnaires regarding feelings of anxiety about poor performance on tests in school.[1] Girls consistently expressed more anxiety about failure than did boys. It has been argued that these results reflect differences in the willingness to admit to fear rather than real differences in the actual fear of failure. Nevertheless, I agree with psychologists Aletha Stein and Margaret Bailey, who, in an extensive review of the research on the development of achievement orientation in women, conclude that a variety of data support the idea that females do indeed have a greater fear of failure than males.[2]

Another line of research suggests that girls have more fear of failure than boys because girls are less likely to learn ways to handle failure. In a study that followed children from childhood to adulthood, psychologists found that girls who have high levels of fear of failure in childhood will continue to have high levels of fear of failure in adulthood. On the other hand, a boy with a high fear of failure as a child may or may not have a high fear of failure as an adult.[3]

These results suggest that, in the process of growing up, boys more than girls have experiences that can change the intensity of their fear of failure. The experiences that allow boys to manage their fear successfully are those that teach boys adaptive responses to failure.

RESPONDING TO FAILURE

Although nobody enjoys failing, some people manage to survive the experience better than others. The survivors tend to respond in a mastery-oriented way: They see failure as a part of a learning process that will allow them to do better the next time around. *Those who respond to failure helplessly are more devastated by it and consequently more afraid of it.*

In reviewing research, psychologists Carol Dweck and Carol Licht found that girls were more helpless in responding to failure initially and less resilient in recovering from it after the fact.[4] Girls appeared to carry over the effects of failure, such as lowered expectations of success, into new situations. Even under changed conditions that should prompt optimism, girls' lowered expectations didn't bounce back up. Once the experience of failure brought them down, the girls had trouble making a comeback. And even when the girls did express confidence about future performance, the confidence was fragile and easily dissipated. Clearly, the helpless girls hadn't learned to take failure in stride.

We learn to have a constructive view of failure by taking action and acquiring the mastery orientation. Consider an example from a self-defense class for women. In the first meeting of the class, the male instructor walks around the room and periodically pulls a chair out from under some unsuspecting woman. With little grace and even less aplomb, she lands on the floor. To learn what? To learn that it's okay to fall down. You pull yourself together and get up again. In the same way, a failure isn't the end of the line. It's only one out in a game that lasts a lifetime.

Those of us who respond poorly to failure do so because we haven't learned to think about failure in adaptive ways. To begin with, as small children we learned that failure means you did something wrong. Doing something wrong means you are bad. Ergo, failure equals badness.

Needless to say, badness is a danger to little girls, who are encouraged to be sugar and spice and everything nice. It poses a threat to obtaining adult approval and to our status as good girls. As a result, some of us find the thought of failure intolerable and come to fear it greatly.

Little boys also equate failure with badness. But, due to differences in sex role socialization, boys have more opportunity to outgrow this notion and acquire a view of failure that allows them to respond to it more resiliently.

Boys learn to value challenge, as well as the courage and struggle needed to meet it, which are glorified by the male culture. That's why we have *Rocky* and *Rocky II* and even *Rocky V*. As boys grow up, they are exposed to such role models and are pressured to strive and to test themselves. They develop the desire to seek out and master new challenges. This urge makes men climb Mt. Everest without oxygen and sail solo around the world in a nine-foot boat.

This frame of mind requires the mastery orientation, with its constructive interpretation of failure. Since by definition a challenge isn't a sure thing and some failure is inevitable, failure must be viewed as a temporary setback that creates an opportunity to learn. It becomes a cue to try something else, not a signal to withdraw. Sustained effort in the face of setbacks allows one to persist long enough to succeed. This in turn reinforces a more optimistic attitude toward future failures.

Males learn these lessons, most dramatically, through fights and sports. On sandlots and street corners, boys learn they have to bounce back. You win some, you lose some. For them, although they may not like it, failure becomes part of the game. Boys must learn these lessons. Their self-esteem and social survival depend on it.

If boys get too much of this, girls get too little. Playing with dolls and crocheting shawls doesn't teach us to land on our cans with style and pop back up with vim and vigor. As we have already seen, the traditionally feminine life-style shields us from failure. Others excuse us from challenge and we learn to excuse ourselves. If we feel intimidated by the abstractions of math and the intricacies of science, it's okay to pass up those subjects. People don't really expect such analytical thinking from us anyway. As one bright underachiever who is afraid of failure put it, "I didn't take on subjects that I didn't think I could do well in, like science. I could get away with it. No one told me otherwise." She took few risks and had few failures—at least in the short run. But, like many others, she didn't learn that one need not be afraid of failure. Not only can we survive it, we can learn from it and grow.

The Helpless Response

One way to think of fear of failure is that it's the anxiety generated by the possibility of failure combined with the anticipation of a helpless response. Although we have already talked about helplessness, the helpless response to failure is so important that it's worth looking at it in detail.

Dweck and Licht reviewed the research that compared the helpless response to failure with the mastery-oriented response.[5] Although the research was conducted with schoolchildren, the thinking patterns of the helpless children are very similar to the thinking patterns of adults who get stuck. Additionally, the comparison between the mastery-oriented and the helpless response is valuable as a practical guide of do's and don'ts.

In these studies, children were asked to solve puzzles that involved tests of discrimination and logic similar to those used in aptitude and achievement tests. At the beginning of the study, all the children were at the same level of ability. Their performance on the tests was similar in terms of speed, accuracy, and sophistication of problem-solving strategy. But once they were confronted with failure, there was a parting of the ways. On encountering difficulty, some children's performance improved, while other children's performance deteriorated. Some were so disrupted by failure that they became incapable of solving the *same* problems they had solved only minutes earlier.

The differences among these children were in their attitudes toward failure. In order to learn more about these differences, researchers asked the children to think out loud as they were working on the puzzles.[6] The study was designed to ensure that each child would initially experience success and then experience failure. The results were fascinating.

While they were experiencing success, the thoughts of all the children were similar. But once the failure began, clear differences in thinking patterns emerged between the helpless and the mastery-oriented children.

As mistakes became apparent, the helpless children labeled their errors as failures sooner than did the mastery-oriented children. Although the mastery-oriented children acknowledged their mistakes, they viewed their errors as temporary mishaps that would be remedied shortly.

The helpless children not only labeled their mistakes as failures prematurely, they went one step further. They attempted to account for their errors. They attributed their failures to lack of ability—"I never did have a good memory"[7]—or they attributed their failures to loss of ability, such as getting confused. Instead of trying to correct their mistakes, the helpless children became preoccupied with the fact that they had made mistakes and with trying to account for them. And their explanation sealed their fates: There wasn't anything they could do about lack of ability.

The mastery-oriented children, on the other hand, didn't waste time worrying about why the mistakes happened. They didn't attempt to account for failure because they didn't see errors as failures. They devoted their time and energy to trying to figure out how to correct the mistakes.

As the helpless children began to err, they developed negative feelings about the puzzles and wanted to stop working on them. They said things like "This isn't fun anymore."[8] They began to shift their attention away from the task. They started talking about things that weren't related to the puzzles. One helpless child said, "There is a talent show this weekend, and I am going to be Shirley Temple."[9]

In marked contrast, as the mastery-oriented children noticed their mistakes, they became more positive about the task. They expressed pleasure at being challenged. They maintained a sense of optimism that their errors would be corrected and they would ultimately succeed. The mastery-oriented children became more rather than less involved in their work. They maintained an ongoing dialogue with themselves about the best way to proceed. They gave themselves instructions and pep talks. They said such things as "I should slow down and try to figure this out" and "The harder it gets, the harder I need to try"[10]

While the helpless children dwelled on their current lack of success and wanted to quit, the mastery-oriented children focused on future success and wanted to try harder. Only after they had exhausted all efforts did the mastery-oriented children label their efforts as failures that needed to be accounted for. But even then, they thought differently. The mastery-oriented children attributed their failure to lack of effort. They didn't devalue their ability; they simply decided that they hadn't worked hard enough.

What was even more intriguing was that the experience of failure caused the helpless children to inflate their failure. When asked, they overestimated the number of problems they hadn't solved. The failure appears to have totally obscured their previous success, which they seemed to forget or consider irrelevant. They didn't use their previous success to predict future success. When asked if they could repeat earlier success, only 65 percent of the helpless children thought that they could.

All the mastery-oriented children thought that they could repeat their earlier success. Unlike the helpless children, they were able to maintain their optimism in the face of failure.

The helpless response to mistakes occurs repeatedly in daily life. Consider the case of Julie, a twenty-five-year-old secretary employed by a group of holistic health practitioners. Although she enjoyed working with people and the stimulation of a medical environment, she felt limited by her role as a secretary. Inspired by the holistic approach, she decided to apply to graduate programs in nutritional sciences. To give herself a head start, she took a course in physiology. The course was rough, far more demanding than her previous undergraduate courses had been.

But the real problem was that Julie responded to difficulty with helplessness. When she didn't understand something in class, she stopped listening. Her mind wandered. She started wondering if she didn't have a head for science. She tended to think that either you have it or you don't. What if she didn't have it? What if she couldn't get into graduate school? What would happen to her future? Was she destined to be a failure? How could she live with it? Julie was off and running.

Like the helpless children, Julie began paying attention to irrelevant matters. She focused on her presumed lack of ability and got lost in wild catastrophic fantasies. She made herself unnecessarily miserable by discounting her ability and panicking about future achievement.

But the problem didn't end there. Because she stopped listening, her mind was closed to additional information. When she stopped taking notes, she further reduced her ability to help herself in the future. Due to her helpless response, her psychological distress was snowballing into tangible real-life problems.

Had Julie been more mastery oriented, she might have reacted differently. She might have jotted down a note to remind herself that certain material needed further clarification. If appropriate, she might have asked the instructor a question. If not, she could have continued listening and taking notes, trying to pick up the lost threads as she went along. Had she done this, she would have increased her chances of learning the material and she would have been much less miserable.

For those of us like Julie, inclined toward helplessness, mistakes, errors, snafus, screw-ups, difficulties, problems, and failures all become signals to stop. In contrast, for the mastery-oriented person, these are signals to do something else. They are cues to pay more attention, to work harder and smarter. Same cues, very different responses.

Some people make things even worse for themselves. They add insult to injury by getting angry at themselves for their mistakes. They call themselves stupid, incompetent, and lamebrained. And they don't stop with a few nasty words. They chew on their mistakes for hours, sometimes even for days and weeks. For them, errors become a signal to stop trying and to start beating on themselves.

FROM THE FRYING PAN INTO THE FIRE

When fear of failure is combined with certain other behavior patterns, a particularly intense and troublesome form of anxiety can result. For people who get stuck, the elements that turn a headache into a migraine are: (1) a split self-image, (2) preoccupation with approval, and (3) all-or-nothing thinking.

Split Self-Image

Most of us have encountered the female student who consistently worries herself to death about a grade and then ends up getting an A.

When our picture of our abilities isn't well integrated, confusion can arise because the split self-image simultaneously produces high and low expectations. While our positive self-image is creating lofty visions of achievement, the negative one is sweeping up the gutter. This makes predicting results difficult. We hope for the best while fearing the worst and end up without clear expectations. The unpredictability of this situation adds considerably to our anxiety because we can't realistically prepare ourselves for any outcome.

In one sense, this anxiety is an expression of uncertainty in an unpredictable situation. But in a broader sense, the anxiety is the result of an ongoing battle between positive and negative views of our ability. At each potential confrontation with failure, we worry that the negative view will be confirmed. Anxiety serves the purpose of protecting the positive self-image from a surprise attack. While it succeeds at this mission, it takes its toll.

Approval

Some of us are excessively concerned with obtaining the approval of others. More than many people, we are playing to an audience. The audience usually consists of real people in our lives, such as family and friends, and a fantasy in our head that is usually a composite of all those who have been important influences on our achievement strivings.

We get wrapped up in pleasing because of our dependence on positive feedback. Positive strokes are important, not only because they feel good but because they validate our ability. They reassure us that we are competent and contradict our negative voices. As one woman put it, "I want people to think I am smart and effective. If they are thinking it, it's true. I want it to be true." Without applause, this woman won't believe in herself.

We are also anxious about negative responses from others. We worry excessively about hisses and boos. We imagine that there are terrible consequences of audience disfavor. There are several common fantasies of what will happen if the audience doesn't like the show. One fantasy is that we will be abandoned. The audience will walk out during intermission and never come back—leaving us alone and unloved. A second is that they will humiliate us. One woman imagined that everyone she knew would circle around her, point their fingers at her, and laugh. A third nightmare is that we will be exposed as frauds. Everyone will see that the emperor isn't wearing any clothes. Our true incompetence will be exposed to the world.

There are serious problems with this theatrical production. Not only is it painful, it's irrelevant. We waste time and energy by staring into space instead of focusing on the nitty-gritty details of what needs to be done. This won't get the job done. Worrying about approval this way is unproductive and inhibits action.

The audience is forgotten in emergencies, where people find the courage of desperation. If the house is on fire, we don't worry what the neighbors will think; we concentrate on putting out the fire. This type of crisis reaction accounts for much procrastination. By waiting until the last minute, we create such an urgent situation that we essentially set a fire under ourselves. We back ourselves into a corner where we must ignore the audience and focus on the task. It works, but it's a stressful and ineffective way to deal with the audience.

When we are excessively concerned about the opinions of others, we are candidates for anxieties that will fuel strong fears of failure.

All-or-Nothing Thinking

When we evaluate ourselves and our experiences in all-or-nothing terms, we see things as all good or all bad. We miss the shades of gray that exist in between. Here are examples of all-or-nothing thinking that came out of the mouths—spoken in earnest—of talented and otherwise intelligent women. One stated, "Anything less than complete success is failure. Nothing in between." Another commented, "To be smart, you must know it all." A third said, "I fear I am going to starve if I make less than twenty-five thousand dollars a year."

Imagine giving yourself a report card and accepting only an A+ as a passing grade, regarding any grade below that as a failure. As unreasonable as this sounds, this is the effect of all-or-nothing thinking. It functions as a pass/fail system where the requirements are so stringent that passing is extremely difficult.

The all-or-nothing mindset makes mountains out of molehills. Sitting down to write the best paper is more intimidating than sitting down to write an acceptable one. When our brain doesn't register the possibility of a lower but still passing grade, we automatically and uncritically assume that our task is to produce a magnificent work. By defining success so narrowly and failure so broadly, we have stacked the odds against ourselves and increased the perceived risks. When we are motivated to succeed, such a setup arouses strong anxieties about failure.

IMPACT

Fear of failure can have a powerful impact on action and achievement. People with strong fears of failure often go to great lengths to avoid the experience of having failed. Two sets of strategies accomplish this: superstriving and avoidance. Some people use one set over the other, while other people use both sets at different times.

Some of us attempt to avoid the experience of failure through a monumental effort to ensure success. We set extremely high standards and work tirelessly to live up to them. The reward for relentless striving is often success— from an objective perspective. But we pay a high price in terms of excessive work and stress. At some point, that price may take its toll in further progress.

Lynn is a superstriver who, despite being a successful lawyer, is unhappy at her work. Lynn works twice as hard as anyone else. She expects herself to be the best and does her darnedest to live up to that expectation. She knocks her brains out trying to work within the constraints of ridiculous deadlines and won't allow herself to proceed at a comfortable pace because she regards that as inefficient. She is afraid that if she relaxes she won't be any good. On the other hand, because she is so compulsive, everything takes longer than necessary. To make matters worse, she doesn't know when to stop and continues working long after diminishing returns have set in. She fears that if she stops too soon she will fail.

Lynn's superstriving affects her relationships as well as her work. She feels lonely in the office. Convinced that socializing interferes with efficiency, she discourages chit-chat. Not only won't she waste precious time chewing the fat, she gets annoyed when others do. She regards the fact that others don't work as hard as she does as an injustice. And because her salary isn't commensurate with her superhuman efforts, she feels exploited. Clearly, Lynn is paying too high a price for her success.

Whereas superstriving promotes action, avoidance impedes it. When ambitious people who fear failure take this route, they invariably wind up feeling miserable and stuck.

On the face of it, avoidance doesn't make any sense. Since it's likely to contribute to failure, why should it be such a popular strategy for dealing with fear of failure? Its attraction lies in the fact that it permits us to maintain a positive self-image by discrediting any given performance as a valid indicator of our ability. We can perform at various levels of competence without fully testing ourselves.

Through this sleight of hand we can indefinitely postpone confronting the limits of our ability and challenging our most cherished visions of our skills and talents.

There are several time-honored forms of avoidance: (1) not doing, (2) playing it safe, (3) limiting investment, and (4) not finishing.

The simplest way of avoiding confrontation with failure is by not trying anything. Taking no action reduces the risk factor to zero: we don't send a tape of our singing to an agent, we don't volunteer our ideas, we don't apply for a fellowship. The problem with this strategy is that, while we may not fail, we can't succeed.

Avoiding challenge is a more subtle way of preventing the experience of failure. We can play it safe by shunning new experiences and sticking with the tried and true. Or we can keep our level of aspiration well below our capabilities and set goals in which success is guaranteed. Choosing the most lenient professors, majoring in easy subjects, following undemanding career paths—all of these are classics in the art of avoiding challenge.

In limiting our investments, we choose appropriate goals (nothing embarrassingly easy or blatantly unachievable) but we don't give them our all. We don't give the task enough time, energy, or money. While this may undermine success, it provides a ready out. A woman who felt unable to get herself going in a potentially successful business described herself this way: "I am the kind of person who doesn't study for an exam for fear of failing. If I do fail I can console myself by saying that I didn't really try."

Another woman described a more subtle pattern of holding back. After she ran for office in a school board election, she said of herself: "I did the same thing with my campaign that I did with my grades in school. I worked very hard and then at the last minute I let up. I never quite got everything done that needed to be done. I never had the feeling that I was really prepared." When we aren't fully prepared, it's easy to dismiss a poor performance as an inaccurate measure of ability.

Procrastination is another favorite way of limiting investment. Scared of doing badly, we put things off until the last moment. That was Julie's strategy for handling physiology: "I was intimidated by physiology and I was scared of the exam. So, I avoided studying. I studied at the last minute. I planned to study before that but I watched television instead." That's what many of us do. We watch television, go out for pizza, wash our hair. We will do almost anything to put off biting the bullet and doing the work. When God is on our side, we can pull it out of the fire in the last minute. When God isn't on our side, we have a ready-made excuse. Our ability hasn't really been tested because our attempt was halfhearted: too little, too late.

Last, but not least, we can attempt to dodge the feeling of failure by not finishing. Some of us drift away from projects, vaguely losing interest. Others deliberately stop. One woman with a talent for art didn't finish her paintings. If she liked what she had done, she stopped for fear of ruining it. She preferred sketching because "a sketch is never really finished." Not surprisingly, she eventually gave up her art.

An unfinished product gets a grade of Incomplete. It isn't an F, it isn't an A. An Incomplete doesn't get evaluated. It leaves the judgment of the performance hanging in midair. No one knows for sure what the grade would have been had the work been completed. Thus, a subjective sense of failure is averted because the audience hasn't been permitted to pass judgment. No catcalls, no hisses, no boos. No roses either, but at least we have cut our losses.

Even when the Incomplete turns into an F by default, our ability hasn't been evaluated. We haven't confronted the limits of our ability and the positive half of our self-image remains untarnished. It boils down to: no finish, no failure.

Any way you slice it, a strong fear of failure can block achievement. Encumbered by it, we feel miserable and stuck. Unshackled by it, we can use our talents and our resources to the best of our ability.

CHAPTER 5

Self-Assertion

*O*ur fame and fortune, not to mention what we do and how we do it, depend on how we get along with people. Relationships can make or break us. This is most apparent in certain fields, such as sales, where relating to others is the first order of business. But even where meeting and greeting isn't the main event, influencing people may be crucial to getting a job done.

A key to effective relationships is self-assertion: the positive expression, by word or deed, of one's rights, thoughts, feelings, desires, and abilities. Or, to put it another way, it's the positive presentation and protection of oneself. Skills in self-assertion aid action, and difficulties with it contribute enormously to getting stuck.

ASSERTION PROBLEMS

In my first year of graduate school I was discussing a research project with a male professor. Since we needed information from another faculty member, the two of us walked over to her office. Her door was closed, so I gave it a few gentle taps. Although this happened long ago, I can still hear my professor's words: "That's no way to knock on a door. No one will take a knock like that seriously." Then he proceeded to pound on the door.

Assertive behavior has traditionally belonged to the male domain. Many of us weren't socialized to speak up, toot our own horns, and defend ourselves; we were brought up to be docile and modest, especially when relating to men. Now that the rules of the game have changed, many women have problems with assertion and these interfere with their achievement. Areas that typically cause women difficulty are: (1) presenting oneself positively, (2) participating in groups, (3) asking and demanding, (4) saying no, (5) confronting, and (6) asserting authority.

Presenting Oneself Positively

A manager working for the Social Security Commission wanted to move into private industry. Being particularly interested in the field of finance, she arranged—through a friend of a friend—a lunch with a stock market analyst for the purpose of learning more about that business. She successfully handled herself by breaking the ice with chitchat and asking intelligent questions about finance. But when he asked her about herself, she fumbled. She described her own work in the most perfunctory manner and quickly turned the conversation back to finance. Later, she felt like kicking herself for missing an opportunity to present herself well.

Presenting ourselves positively is conveying the fact that we are smart, talented, and can do the job. It's letting people know that we are competent *and* we know it. In tangible, behavioral terms it means being able to talk positively about our abilities and accomplishments in a comfortable, matter-of-fact manner with as much detail as is permissible; speaking with voice quality, facial expressions, and body language that reinforce the content of the message; hiding nervousness and self-doubt under a rock.

This type of presentation helps get things done. We must be credible; other people must have faith in our competence. If we don't put on a good show, no one will buy our act. Women often feel inhibited about talking positively about themselves. We often neglect to claim recognition that is rightfully ours. Even when we do talk about ourselves, we talk about our abilities and accomplishments too briefly, too vaguely, and too passively.

When we do acknowledge our assets, we frequently feel anxious, awkward, and uncomfortable. Dr. Pamela Butler, a psychologist who conducts assertiveness training groups for professional women, routinely asks women to introduce themselves in a positive manner. She finds that this exercise causes more anxiety than all other group exercises combined.[1]

This anxiety is caused by a sense that we are violating social rules. We have a vague feeling that we are behaving inappropriately. A woman with a master's degree in business administration from Harvard told me, "I don't like to mention Harvard because it makes me feel pretentious." A powerful manager in an important company who was talking about her desire to make changes was saying, "I have a lot of ideas on how to reorganize this company." Then she stopped abruptly, looked embarrassed, and said, "I feel very pompous saying that."

The rules that many women are afraid of violating are those against bragging. While tolerated in men, bragging is unacceptable in women. It flies in the face of feminine behavior: Not only is it immodest, it's self-centered and self-serving.

Since bragging is such an affront to traditional femininity, the proscriptions against it have a particularly powerful effect on women. In our zeal to be modest and unassuming, many of us have learned to equate talking positively about ourselves with bragging.

Not all self-enhancing statements are bragging. Bragging is a specific type of communication. It is self-enhancing content combined with hostility and inappropriateness. It is a hostile competitive maneuver in situations where hostile competitiveness is uncalled for.

Positive remarks about ourselves don't imply hostility or inappropriateness; they can be factual statements that convey information about competence. If you are asked to talk about yourself and you say positive things, that isn't bragging. If you volunteer information about your talents and accomplishments in appropriate situations, that isn't bragging. Conveying information clearly and fully when suitable isn't bragging.

Holding back, self-minimization, and excessive modesty aren't the opposites of bragging. They are forms of ineffectual communication. Effective communication for achievement means presenting ourselves positively.

Participating in Groups

A woman executive, recently hired, attended her first board meeting at corporate headquarters. Being new to the company, she said little. At the end of the meeting, a senior executive took her aside and said, "If you don't speak up more, people will assume you are a secretary."

From the boardroom to the scientific laboratory to the dance troupe, achieving goals often hinges on having power in groups. When lack of assertiveness results in ineffective group participation, it can interfere with gaining the influence needed for accomplishment.

Dr. Gerald Phillips, a sociologist, and Dr. Eugene Erickson, a communications expert, pooled their knowledge of group interaction and came up with some useful generalizations about how groups operate.[2] They found that speaking up, asserting oneself, is the key to participating effectively and gaining influence. Because the action in groups centers around its more vocal members, they are the ones who tend to dominate the decision-making process. The more people can overcome their awkwardness about expressing themselves, the greater their chances of having an impact.

Group members who are extremely unassertive, who withdraw from the group action, usually get ignored. Remarks aren't addressed to them. Their wishes aren't taken into account. When they do attempt to speak, they are fair game for interruption. Often they are heard out politely and then passed over—regardless of the merits of their comments. Their lack of participation is taken as a signal that they are either uninterested in or incapable of contributing to the group.

When women and men are together in groups, women participate less.[3] To begin with, women talk less. They make fewer and briefer comments. Beyond that, however, there is a difference in the type of input women make. Women tend to make supportive rather than task-oriented comments. They are more likely to praise the suggestions of others than to contribute their own ideas. Women are less likely than men to assert opinions, provide information, and offer solutions to problems. Even when women do make task-oriented remarks, they are less likely to support and defend their own ideas. One study found that while men supported their own ideas 75 percent of the time, women supported their own ideas only 40 percent of the time.[4]

The implications of this research call out. If we don't assert ourselves by sharing our information, ideas, and opinions with fluency and conviction, we will have little power and status in groups. To the extent that we need this influence in order to accomplish our goals, our lack of assertiveness will undermine our ability to achieve.

Asking and Demanding

Mary Beth came for counseling because she was miserable at her job and couldn't decide whether to change jobs. One cause of her misery was that she worked hard but found that her colleagues had more fun and more job perks. While they were getting tuition reimbursements, free dinners when they worked late, and extra vacation time when they worked above and beyond the call of duty, Mary Beth was feeling overworked and unappreciated. In analyzing the problem, she realized that "the people who get are the ones who ask." She also realized that she had difficulty asking. Like Mary Beth, many of us have difficulty making requests. Demanding—asking insistently or authoritatively—is even harder.

The worst problem is asking for ourselves. Although we may be able to ask on behalf of others, we feel inhibited about asking that others give *to us*. As women we aren't supposed to pay much attention to our own needs and wishes. We are supposed to give to others. Actively pursuing our own desires, behavior perfectly acceptable in men, is often regarded as selfish, pushy, and unattractive in women. As a result, many of us feel uncomfortable and vaguely inappropriate in asking for ourselves. As Mary Beth put it, "It's like asking for flowers."

Another problem comes from a notion that many of us were brought up with—if you are a good girl things will naturally go your way. If you work hard and do well, you will be justly rewarded. This leads some of us to assume (sometimes subconsciously) that if we do good work, rewards will automatically be forthcoming. Consequently it doesn't occur to us to ask, and we find ourselves waiting to be taken care of.

While the strategy of being good and waiting for Santa may work for adorable little girls at Christmastime, it doesn't work for big girls out in the real world. In the real world, you have to go after what you want. People who get ahead are able to open their mouths and let their wishes be known. They are able to ask for jobs, money, recognition, promotions, opportunities, office space, office furniture, tuition reimbursement, support services, expense accounts, and anything else they require. Sometimes plums fall into people's laps, but don't hold your breath.

As business consultant Betty Harragan, author of *Games Mother Never Taught You*, wrote, "The secret of success is to ask, and keep asking."[5]

Saying No

One of the most difficult types of self-assertion for women is saying no. Saying no means putting ourselves first and others second—placing us in direct conflict with the values of traditional femininity.

If you're "just a girl who can't say no" you may have trouble at the office. Consider Millie, who works for the telephone company. One of her primary responsibilities is coordinating requests for service with the technicians who install and repair equipment. Millie spends a great deal of her time on the telephone trying to solve an endless series of problems. She is always behind in her paperwork because whenever the phone rings, which is all the time, she drops what she is doing and gives the caller's problem her immediate attention. In reality, most of these calls could wait, but Millie is perpetually trying to do the impossible. She never feels on top of things and is chronically frustrated.

When we don't say no, for all practical purposes we are saying yes. As long as we don't set limits on others' demands, we are putting out the welcome mat. Not only are we giving the okay in a particular situation, we may be conveying the message that our door is always open. This will encourage them to keep knocking. If we want the knocking to stop, we have to say no.

The inability to deny the requests of others renders us unable to protect our resources of time, energy, and enthusiasm. Many women who have complained about their work described precisely this type of situation. Like Millie, they were overworked, frustrated, anxious, and exhausted. The stress spilled over into their personal lives. They became so preoccupied with their impossible jobs they were unable to enjoy their leisure time.

Setting priorities is the one way of protecting our resources. This means saying yes to some tasks and no to others. Right now I will do this and *not* that. People who can't say no often have trouble setting priorities. Just as we have difficulty refusing Tom's direct request, we may have difficulty delaying Tom's task until a more opportune moment. The more our tasks are connected directly to others, the more our inability to say no can undermine our work.

Confronting

"Foul!" shouts the umpire. In the same way, we sometimes need to call others on their actions. We find ourselves in situations where we have to ask others to change their behavior.

This type of request has the potential for arousing opposition or antagonism. Often when we contemplate confrontations, we anticipate an unpleasant reaction: anger, disapproval, dislike, or rejection. Although these responses aren't inevitable, they are distinct possibilities.

Most people don't like confrontations. Women, in particular, are often frightened of them. The idea of confronting others suggests an aggressiveness that conflicts with the fragile and compliant image of traditional femininity. And for some of us, the thought of disapproval is so painful that we will go miles out of our way to avoid it.

Confrontations are inevitable. There are countless situations in which one person must challenge the actions of another. In the following examples, women considered the option of confrontation.

- A nursing supervisor was faced with a disrupted ward because of the poor work and attitudes of some nurses' aides.
- A sociologist was collaborating on a book with her former mentor, who wasn't holding up his end of the collaboration and was delaying publication.
- An executive in an international corporation was angered by her new superior, a vice president recently transferred from a European office, who ignored the chain of command. He gave orders to her subordinates without discussing it with her or even informing her about it.

Whether or not to call people on their actions is a practical and political matter. But in order to make sound decisions, we must have the option of confrontation. If we are unable to confront, we automatically close off a valuable course of action.

Asserting Authority

"I have a hard time giving orders. I don't do it well. I have arranged my life so I don't have to give them." These are the words of a financial analyst who is struggling with achievement issues.

Research suggests that other women in the work force also have difficulty giving orders. In one study, questionnaires were filled out by 254 executives who were supervising businesswomen in *Fortune* 500 companies.[6] There were several areas in which women's performance was below what their supervisors desired. Delegating workloads was one of the biggest problems.

If presenting ourselves positively is tough, asserting authority is even tougher. Not only do we have to let people know that we are competent, we have to convey the impression that we are in charge and entitled to lead. The problem is that to convince others we have to believe it ourselves or, at the very least, fake it successfully.

Many of us have trouble believing we are entitled to direct others because men are supposed to lead and direct, women are supposed to follow and submit. As a result, some of us feel there is a conflict between authority and femininity. Some of us are so unassertive that we have difficulty asserting authority over anyone. Others have particular difficulty in asserting authority over men. We tend to regard asserting authority over men (particularly those close to our own social status) as inappropriate and a threat to our sense of femininity.

The power of this notion was demonstrated in a piece of research. A psychologist grouped people into pairs and asked them to decide which member of the pair would be the leader.[7] The pairs weren't picked at random; the participants were grouped according to scores on a test of dominance that they had taken earlier. Each pair consisted of one person high in dominance and one person low in it. Given this setup, one would expect that the more dominant person would emerge as leader. This is, in fact, what happened in 70 percent of the cases in which both members of the pair were of the same sex.

On the other hand, when the pair consisted of a man and a woman, some dramatic differences emerged. When a highly dominant male was paired with a less dominant female, the male emerged as leader 90 percent of the time.

But when a highly dominant female was paired with a less dominant male, the female emerged as leader only 20 percent of the time. Even more intriguing, though, is the fact that in the majority of the cases, the highly dominant women made the decision to elect the man as leader. Clearly, sex role conventions overrode individual differences in personality most of the time.

Authority is a masculine concept because in our society most authority figures have been male. Only in the limited spheres of raising and educating children have women been allowed to control the behavior of others. Although social conditions have begun to change, this is still more true than not. We lack sufficient female role models for leadership in the larger world. As a result, when it comes to asserting authority, many of us have a gap in our concept of authority, our self-image, and our behavioral repertoire.

ASSERTIVENESS SKILLS

The process of self-assertion can be broken down into individual components: knowing what to say, matching verbal and nonverbal behavior, controlling tension, and knowing when to assert.

It's hard to be assertive when at a loss for words. In order to speak up effectively, we need to decide what we want to say and the best way to pitch it. We have to find the right words and arrange them in a reasonable order. The importance of good wording is most obvious in delicate negotiations such as asking for a raise. But even in less dramatic situations, thoughts expressed in clear, fluent language tend to have the most impact.

Imagine trying to assert authority with your head hanging, shoulders slumped, and eyes focused on a crack in the floor. That's a blueprint for being disregarded.

As every politician and actor knows, people are influenced by more than just persuasive arguments. We all pay attention to other bits of information about a speaker. In fact, sometimes we pay more attention to nonverbal signals; facial expression, eye movement, voice tone and volume, posture, hand motions, and dress all give out strong messages. When these are moving together harmoniously, a convincing manner is presented. When the words and the music don't come together, the performance isn't taken seriously.

One way to create this harmony is to manage tension. Tension interferes with communication. It can disrupt the smooth flow of words and betray vulnerability. To compound matters, it can be contagious. Discomfort can be transmitted back and forth until everyone is ready to jump out of their skin. This makes doing business an obstacle course.

People who are unassertive often have difficulty in knowing when to open their mouths and when to keep them shut. Feeling unentitled to assert themselves, they question the appropriateness of speaking up in situations where others wouldn't give it a second thought. But because they have trouble making these distinctions and know that they err on the side of being unassertive, they sometimes imagine that they should be speaking up when, in fact, they should be quiet. Even women with a lot of savvy sometimes have difficulty distinguishing between an assertion problem and a political one.

If someone is literally stepping on your toes and you say nothing, that's an assertiveness problem. But if someone is "stepping on your toes" by posing a threat to your power, self-esteem, or efficiency, that's a political problem and the solution is more complicated than saying "Please get off my foot." Before you say anything, you have to size up (sometimes very quickly and almost subconsciously) the overall situation and figure out what makes sense in terms of long-range goals. If it's politically expedient to roll over and play dead, that isn't unassertiveness, that's pragmatism. But if assertion is called for and you don't speak up, that's an assertion problem.

To make these types of distinctions, it helps to know the formal and informal rules of your game: the moves you are required and entitled to make, when your interests are threatened, and the rewards and punishments of your political system.

One manager appreciated the fact that her office—its size, location, and furnishings—was an important piece in her corporate game. Having accepted a position with a company, she arrived on her first day of work to discover that not only didn't she have the same spacious office of her predecessor, she was moved to a cubicle in a more isolated section of the building. Perceiving this office switch to be an ominous sign of her future power, she felt she had no choice but to speak up. If she didn't meet this challenge head-on she was going to start work with a handicap from which she might never recover.

Not all of us have a clear grasp of political realities. To some of us the subtleties of the working world are as unfamiliar as the dark side of the moon. One bright young businesswoman who was a pioneer in a macho man's business said repeatedly with great dismay, "I can't believe it. There are no rules out there. Anything goes."

Visitors to a foreign land full of strange customs, we don't always know which fork to use. But it's possible to learn the rules and rituals, and when we do, it will be easier to figure out when and how to assert ourselves.

IMPACT

Assertiveness or lack of it can make a big difference in our level of accomplishment and satisfaction with our work. Lack of assertiveness can undermine effectiveness, invite exploitation, lower self-esteem, encourage avoidance, and contribute to confusion.

If we don't request, refuse, and confront, people won't know what we want and expect and we will be less likely to get it. If we don't present ourselves positively and share opinions and ideas, we will be less influential.

Although unassertive people sometimes complain of feeling ineffectual, they often don't realize how their effectiveness has been compromised until they begin asserting themselves more.

An extremely unassertive research assistant took a course in public speaking and was told that she spoke in a tentative way—as if she didn't expect to be taken seriously. (Something, by the way, according to research, that is more characteristic of women's language than of men's.[8]) Her class felt that she needed to make more definitive, assertive statements. She followed the advice and was delighted with the results. She found that now when she spoke to her secretaries, she was more effective in getting things done. Her typing was done sooner and she didn't have to make the same request several times in order to get compliance. Not only that, the secretaries seemed to be more comfortable and to have more respect for her.

We are sitting ducks for being or feeling exploited when we are unassertive. Some people will inevitably make unacceptable demands. If we don't set limits on these demands, we won't be able to protect our interests and resources. We are likely to put out or put up with more than we desire.

Even when others aren't deliberately trying to take advantage of us, our inability to say no or to request reasonable compensation can leave us feeling resentful and used.

Marge works for a frozen food company. She began as the secretary to the president of the company, and over time she assumed more and more responsibility until she was doing the work of a buyer. While she had the distinction of being the only woman buyer, when she attended business meetings, people still introduced her as the president's secretary. She would fume inside but she did nothing to correct the mistaken impression. She didn't say that she was in charge of buying for an entire division of the company. Instead, as she felt her status being diminished, her self-esteem dropped. She felt badly about herself because she thought that others devalued her and she felt helpless to do anything about it.

Lack of assertiveness, such as Marge's, can cause considerable psychological discomfort. By not speaking up we permit other people to control situations, and in some cases we inadvertently allow ourselves to be devalued. This lowers self-esteem. If this pattern continues over a long period of time, psychological damage can result.

One of the most insidious consequences of unassertive behavior is that it contributes to avoidance. Knowing or sensing their liability, some unassertive people become afraid of situations that require assertion and attempt to avoid them. They avoid phone calls, public speaking, and networking. Sometimes they go out of their way to avoid superiors, colleagues, and subordinates.

Furthermore, tasks associated with assertion can also become targets of avoidance. A common garden-variety phobic reaction that relates to unassertiveness is writing the résumé. Many women have a terrible time trying to sit down and write a résumé. They would rather clean stables. What is so terrifying? Surely not pen and paper. The terror is inspired by a task that demands presenting a glowing picture of one's abilities and accomplishments, and the anticipation of making this presentation in the flesh.

Steering clear of situations that require assertion leads to a vicious cycle. The avoidance interferes with problem solving and mastery. If problems aren't solved and skills aren't acquired, deficits and inhibitions persist. These in turn perpetuate avoidance. The cycle continues, leaving underachievement in its wake.

Some women are quite aware of how avoidance of self-assertion affects their work. One woman reported that often she didn't finish projects because once they were completed, she felt compelled to go out and sell them. She was terrified at the thought of hustling business. Although she had great ideas and loved designing projects, she was stuck because she avoided self-assertion.

Other women aren't as aware of their fears and simply experience what they view as laziness or lack of motivation. One woman expressed it this way: "I have been thinking about my motivation. I am usually not a self-starter. I think maybe it's because I avoid fights and situations where I have to be assertive. I have been doing this all my life. Maybe that's why I don't initiate things." She is quite right. No action, no hassles, no need for assertion.

Still other women experience anxiety, but don't connect it with their fear of assertion. All they know is that in certain situations they are extremely uncomfortable. One woman, very talented in solving the technical problems in her work, was increasingly called upon to do consulting for other companies. She appeared to handle it competently but she hated it. She felt unconfident and wanted to leave her job on account of it.

In the course of discussing the matter, she realized that it was the possibility of having her authority challenged that kept her in a state of perpetual tension while consulting. She was afraid that she wouldn't be able to assert herself if her authority was to be questioned in any way.

Some of us misdiagnose our problems. We imagine we lack confidence because we don't know enough. And sometimes this is the case. But often we are really confusing lack of technical knowledge with lack of assertion skills. It's true that we lack something. But the deficit is in our interpersonal skills, not in our technical know-how. This confusion probably helps account for the fact that women, more than men, want supervision in their work and seek out additional training.

A tip-off to this type of misdiagnosis is when others are surprised by our lack of confidence. If they have faith in our competence when we have serious doubts, there's reason to suspect an assertion problem.

The confusion can be painful because a misdiagnosed problem can't be solved. We can study technical material until the cows come home and still lack confidence. It's like looking for cabbages in Tiffany's. We won't find them.

CAUSES

It helps to understand why we do what we do. There are many reasons for unassertive behavior. The major ones are fear of the consequences, habit, lack of skill, lack of self-knowledge, and low self-esteem.

Eileen, a manager in a computer company, had a new assistant, a charming young man with poor work habits. He didn't know the meaning of the word "punctuality." But what bothered Eileen the most was that he didn't seem to have much regard for the chain of command either. Sometimes he went above and around her as if she didn't exist.

Eileen decided to have a talk with her assistant. But she felt uneasy. After the talk, which went quite smoothly, she still felt uneasy. Was she being too hard on the young man? Was she being picky?

Many women fear that self-assertion will displease others. Because women are so geared to pleasing, the thought of losing approval and affection can be a potent factor in inhibiting self-assertion.

Generally speaking, we are likely to feel inhibited about asserting ourselves when we sense that some type of punishment may result. In addition to loss of approval and affection, we may fear such things as criticism, humiliation, anger, and rejection. Or we may fear looking foolish or stupid, or hurting other people's feelings.

The hazards of self-assertion are both real and imagined. We do run risks when we open our mouth; if we should put our foot into it, we can have psychological, social, or economic loss. But often the feared consequences are projections arising from unrealistic anxieties. Frequently when we assert ourselves, we discover that our fears were groundless.

Another reason many of us don't assert ourselves is habit. As we grow up, we get rewarded for certain types of behavior and punished for others. We watch role models who also give us ideas about how we should act. Over time, we develop behavior patterns that become second nature to us.

We get comfortable with our habits. We get used to being subdued in coed groups, to minimizing our accomplishments, to saying yes regardless of how we feel. Although we may not fear the consequences of doing otherwise, we continue to be unassertive because it's familiar and easy. It takes know-how and effort to do something new.

One behavior pattern that has a powerful effect on assertion in the workplace is the habit of automatically deferring to men. Many of us assume that men are smarter and more knowledgeable. Even when the facts contradict this notion, we somehow believe that men have special powers for dealing with the world. Psychoanalyst Jean Baker Miller writes: "It is not simply that women are obviously excluded from acquiring experience in the serious world of work, but that they actually come to believe that there is some special, inherent ability, some factor that escapes them and must inevitably escape them. . . . Most women have lifelong conditioning that induces them to believe this myth."[9]

This affects our interactions with men. Often we defer too quickly. We don't stop to think independently or to assert our opinions enough of the time. Some of us who don't defer immediately and give the guys a run for their money still believe that men are superior. One woman described herself: "I can't argue with men. I put up a good fight on the outside, but inside the gears in my brain get disengaged. I don't think well. I never win."

Fortunately, this malady is amenable to treatment. One recovering male idealizer described her progress: "I have a tendency to think that men know it all. That they always know more than I do and have the inside track. I used to think that automatically. Not so automatic any more. I am learning to check it."

Some of us don't assert ourselves because we lack some skills. A particular vulnerability for many women is managing the tension that comes with anger. One woman commented on her lack of skill in this area: "I am afraid that when I am angry I will blow it and say what I think. I am afraid I will go for the jugular and then there will be no turning back. That makes me feel vulnerable." Someone else expressed a different concern: "I am afraid I can't control my anger and I will burst into tears."

Because we have been taught that anger is unfeminine and have been encouraged to suppress it, many of us haven't learned to deal with anger effectively. Recognizing our lack of skill in handling anger, we feel uneasy in situations where it's aroused. Afraid of embarrassing ourselves, of being too aggressive or too emotional, we retreat from self-assertion.

It's much easier to assert ourselves when we are sure of who we are and what we want. But this type of self-knowledge is new for many women. Jane is a case in point. Jane's boss, the new editor-in-chief of a computer magazine, didn't feel quite at home in his new position. He wanted information that he knew the source wouldn't want to reveal. So he dumped the problem into Jane's lap, asking that she make the difficult phone call. Jane obliged and was successful.

The editor was delighted and commented on Jane's "persuasive charm." This apparent compliment disconcerted Jane but she didn't know why. After discussing it, she realized that she felt put down by the remark. It wasn't charm that got the information, it was skill. Whatever his intentions, the editor had discounted Jane's negotiating ability.

Jane was slow to figure out how she felt because, in some ways, she didn't know herself well. Her self-image didn't include the concept of skillful negotiator. Without this concept she didn't know how to label what she had done. But at least she was uncomfortable with the label "charm." Had Jane's self-image been better defined, she might have been clearer about her thoughts and feelings and she might have responded more assertively to what she sensed was a put-down.

According to researchers, people who have high self-esteem, all other things being equal, are more likely to be assertive than those with low self-esteem.[10]

When we don't feel good about ourselves we tend to devalue our abilities, thoughts, and feelings. Self-assertion doesn't make much sense to us. Presenting ourselves positively seems dishonest and presumptuous. Asserting authority seems laughable: "Why should anyone take *my* direction?"

A vicious cycle develops. Low self-esteem leads to lack of assertion, which in turn leads to lowered self-esteem.

Anything that decreases our sense of self-worth can affect assertion. Personal problems that make us feel bad about ourselves can interfere with assertiveness on the job. This is particularly likely to happen when assertive behavior isn't a well-established habit. For example, several women who were trying to speak up more at work found themselves backsliding when their love lives turned sour.

Melissa found herself in such a situation. Instead of promoting Melissa to a job that she was already doing to some extent, Tim, Melissa's supervisor, hired a man who, as it turned out, couldn't handle the work. To solve this problem, Tim asked Melissa to do some of her old work. Since she had been working on becoming more assertive, Melissa tactfully declined, feeling content to let Tim stew in his own sexist juices. But Tim's next request came right after Melissa had a devastating fight with her husband. Feeling low and vulnerable, she backed down and agreed to help Tim out. Although she had anticipated the request and had planned to refuse it, she gave in. In her words, "I have been good about assertiveness the last few weeks. But I regressed this time. Old insecurities came rushing back. I felt like a kid again. It showed up in my work."

ASSERTIVENESS TRAINING

For well over a decade, assertiveness training has captured the popular imagination. Books and workshops abound. This "movement" has made considerable contributions: it has focused attention on the problem of self-assertion, analyzed assertive and nonassertive behavior, and developed excellent strategies for helping people change. Moreover, it has recognized and addressed some of the special needs of women. Yet for all these valuable contributions, the basic definition of assertion used by much of the training movement presents some problems for women in the world of work.

A good deal of the time, the term "assertion" has been linked with open, honest, and direct communication. Consider a typical definition from a book for trainers: "Assertion involves standing up for personal rights, and expressing thoughts, feelings, and beliefs in direct, honest, and appropriate ways which do not violate another person's rights."[11]

While one can't argue against the virtues of honest communication, this type of definition muddies the waters. It unnecessarily confounds behavioral description with moral value judgments. It suggests that only direct and honest behavior is assertive. That runs counter to common sense. Assertion and honesty are two different dimensions that don't necessarily go together.

The marriage of assertion and direct honesty has given indirect communication bad press. Manipulation has been regarded as a cardinal sin. But the fact is that in the real world, openness and honesty aren't always standard operating procedure. Manipulation is often the name of the game. The people who gain power are often those who manipulate best, not those who manipulate least.

Although according to dictionary definitions "assertive" and "aggressive" can be used as synonyms—meaning energetic, forceful, bold, or confident—assertiveness trainers have made a major distinction between the two words. They label forceful self-expression that respects the rights of others as assertive, and hostile or domineering self-expression as aggressive.

This distinction is powerful because it gives people who are disinclined to be feisty permission to speak up. It's particularly important for women who live in terror of being aggressive lest they be considered unfeminine. It relieves the fear that being the wicked witch of the west is the only alternative to being a doormat.

But the assertiveness training approach sidesteps an important issue. In some situations, aggressive behavior is rewarded by the environment and unaggressive behavior may be ignored or discounted. This is no minor matter in the world of work.

A textbook editor was asked to go on the road to promote her publication. It was a new ball game for her. Giving presentations in hotel conference rooms provided unexpected challenges. One time she requested that a conference room be set up with a slide projector, a screen, water and glasses, and chairs lined up in rows. When she came to the room five minutes before the meeting, she found the place empty: no chairs, no screen, no projector—nothing. She spoke assertively to several members of the hotel staff and got no satisfaction. Finally this usually genteel woman blew her top. As she described it, "I screamed and out of my mouth came words I didn't know I knew." Her colleagues who had known her for years were flabbergasted. She, herself, was quite stunned. So was the hotel management. Suddenly, as if by magic, the chairs, the slide projector, the screen, and a pitcher of water and glasses materialized out of thin air.

Another woman, a successful pioneer in a traditionally male industry, violates all the rules on how women are supposed to behave. She uses the aggressive language typical of the men in that industry. She sprinkles her speech with such choice tidbits as "Look, you son of a bitch, if you don't get your act together I am going to have your ass in a sling." She may be the only woman who can pull that off, but it works for her.

The point isn't to encourage aggressiveness but to present a dilemma that can't simply be defined away. Making the distinction between aggressiveness and assertiveness solves some problems, but not all of them. To the extent that women want to or are compelled to play in the male leagues, we are faced with basic questions about ourselves and our values. How aggressive, or even ruthless, do we have to be to succeed? Can we do it? Do we want to? Men have been pondering these matters for years. Now we too must confront them.

One of the hazards of emphasizing self-assertion is conveying the idea that assertion is an end in itself. Far from it. It isn't so much that being assertive is so wonderful as it is that being unassertive is so problematic. Problems with assertion hold us back, while the ability to assert allows us to exercise more control over our social environment. It's a tool that helps us develop and exercise our skills to the limits of our motivation and talent.

Part Two

GETTING UNSTUCK

CHAPTER 6

Basics

We have just looked at internal barriers to achievement and how they develop in women. Now that we know *why* we get stuck, how do we stop marking time and start running the great race?

Some of us think that the way to get going is to examine our thoughts and feelings. We imagine that the process of self-exploration, by itself, will break up the logjam and permit smooth sailing. Sometimes this works, but often it doesn't.

Self-exploration is effective when it brings about changes in attitude that result in taking action. Although we need to talk and think, ultimately we must *do* something differently or we will remain stuck. Self-exploration that doesn't bring about action, while fascinating and rewarding in other ways, is of little practical value in solving achievement problems.

The cure for feeling stuck is to take action: to set goals, to make plans for achieving those goals, and to implement the plans deliberately and effectively. Action is the antidote for learned helplessness. It helps to reduce anxiety and depression. It contributes to self-knowledge and to the resolution of internal conflict. Unfortunate myths, such as the innate inferiority of women, get dispelled through action.

The remainder of this book is designed to help people get started and to keep going. Behavioral strategies and techniques are described in detail. But before getting into specifics, let's look at some broader concepts: the mastery assumption, limited commitment, structure, accountability, practice, progress, and support.

THE MASTERY ASSUMPTION

There is a common thread running through the variety of internal obstacles to achievement: learned helplessness. Despite the diversity of the discrete problems, our task—in the broadest sense—is to shift from helpless responses to mastery-oriented ones. Our mission is to challenge our assumptions of uncontrollability. To this end, it's useful to adopt what I call *the mastery assumption*—the idea that there is always something more we can try to improve our situation; the faith that if we knock on enough doors, someone will answer.

For those of us who have learned helplessness, adopting the mastery assumption requires a few mental gymnastics. We start by recognizing that we underestimate our ability to solve certain types of problems. As our expectation of success in these areas is bound to be unrealistically low, we mustn't allow ourselves to accept pessimistic assessments unquestioningly. We should be suspicious of any thoughts that resemble, even remotely, "I can't do it" or "It can't be done." It's best to assume that our estimate of possibilities is always an underestimate. If we see one option, we should assume there are at least three more and set about finding them.

Of course doing this won't guarantee success. However, not doing this is likely to ensure a profound form of failure. Not only won't we solve the problem, we will continue to perpetuate vulnerability to learned helplessness, which will set us up for more failures down the road.

LIMITED COMMITMENT

Carol was working in an impossible situation. Stunned, lonely, and vulnerable after the sudden accidental death of her lover, Carol had an affair with her boss. The affair had run its course and was winding down. Meanwhile, she had gradually assumed more and more responsibility in her job, although her salary and title remained unchanged. This growth inspired the desire for more advancement. But Carol knew that she had reached a dead end. Her once supportive boss had become vindictive. He now alternated between being mildly seductive and subtly abusive. It was driving her crazy. She knew she had to leave. Unfortunately, her self-confidence hadn't increased along with her responsibility. In fact, the lack of recognition and the barrage of abuse raised endless doubts. How could she leave? What else could she possibly do? Who would want her? She thought about résumés, phone calls, hunting for leads, interviews, and her blood ran cold. The task seemed too much for her. She couldn't commit herself to taking on such an overwhelming challenge. Carol was stuck.

Carol was stumbling over one of the first roadblocks on the path to achievement—the idea that one must make a "total commitment" to a particular goal or course of action before taking even one step. Carol imagined that she must be prepared to do it all or not at all.

It isn't surprising that some of us get stuck on the notion of total commitment. It's a central theme in the propaganda used to keep women out of the work force. Women aren't entitled to work or to get top jobs because women don't make a total commitment to their work. While men sell their souls, women simply pass time. They rush off to get married and have children. Money invested in their training gets wasted. Employers are left holding the bag. Ladies, stay home where you belong, has been the message. No wonder some of us think that we must make a total commitment before we do anything at all.

While feeling pressured to make total commitments, women often find it difficult to do so. Total commitments demand a reasonable expectation of success. When we lack confidence, total commitments seem absurd as well as impossible. Failure seems guaranteed. Feeling incapable of doing it all, we do nothing.

But it isn't necessary to make a total commitment. Frequently it's impossible to do so because we can't fully appreciate what we are undertaking. Often, at the beginning, we simply don't have enough experience or information. Total commitment is the outcome of a lengthy process. It grows through action. Total commitment is the final stretch, not the starting line.

When thinking total commitment, we tend to forget that we don't do things in one fell swoop. We achieve goals through a series of small steps. Each has the potential for providing knowledge about our project and about ourselves. Each creates the opportunity to evaluate, to decide whether to stop or go on.

Every step, even seemingly small ones, can change us. With each, we can modify our vision of what is possible. We see things we didn't see before. We get a clearer picture of our goals and the suitability of our plans. We develop new ideas and reject old ones. Perspective changes, and as it changes, so does our ability to make commitments. Step five looks very different from step four than it did before step one. What was inconceivable yesterday becomes remotely possible today and may be "doable" tomorrow.

Commitment usually proceeds in stages. Although we may not pay much attention to the process, we are aware of the critical points at which we question or evaluate our commitments. I recall being acutely aware of making a commitment to writing this book when I invested twenty dollars in typing paper. I wondered what I was going to do with five hundred sheets of erasable bond and half a dozen scratch pads. Was I really going to write a book? Was I wasting my twenty dollars?

Critical points occur when we have to invest more time, more energy, or more money in our project, or when we feel discouraged or are forced to confront fears. Then we start wondering and talking to ourselves. Having come this far, do I want to continue? Is it worth it? Do I really want this? However we phrase it, it's through these periodic struggles that commitment grows.

Our initial commitment can be limited: a pledge to try, to begin, to take a few first steps. No more, no less. We do need an ultimate goal, but only as a guide for current activities, not as an immediate target.

Consider Carol. She was too overwhelmed to make a major commitment to changing jobs. Fortunately, she doesn't need to. She need make only a small commitment to begin the process. She might begin by deciding to review her résumé. If she can get through that, she can *then* decide about taking the next step.

In fact, Carol did begin by reviewing her résumé. She gave thought to all she had done since her last résumé. She wrote down her accomplishments, her strengths, her weaknesses, her likes, her dislikes. After several weeks, she came up with the idea that she liked management. She followed up this idea by reading and networking and then made another limited commitment. She decided to investigate the MBA programs in the area. After several weeks of research, she found there was only one program that interested her. She decided to apply to that one school and made no commitment beyond that. She wasn't ready to make contingency plans in case she wasn't accepted to the program.

These steps were enough to make Carol feel better. Her boss was still difficult, but it didn't bother her as much. One foot was already out the door. She knew that she had a direction and that, when the time came, she would be able to move. Carol was unstuck.

Limited commitments take the pressure off. We need commit ourselves only to whatever we can do right now. The important thing is to find *something* we can do and to make a commitment to doing it.

Lydia is a bright young woman who wanted to be a doctor but had low expectations. She doubted that she had the intelligence, stamina, or discipline to survive medical school. To go or not to go? That was her question. For years she straddled the fence: She neither applied nor gave up her dream.

I suggested to Lydia that she not worry about making a commitment to becoming a doctor. As an alternative, she could make a limited commitment *to apply* to medical school, *not to go* to medical school. Her mission was to complete the application process. Period. If she was accepted, *then* she could decide. If she was rejected, there would be no decision to make.

I assured Lydia that by the time she finished the application process, she would be in a different place. The process of applying would give her important experiences and feedback. This information would change her perspective enough so that she could make a decision.

The idea of a limited commitment appealed to Lydia: She felt as if a weight had been lifted. She began the application process—a seemingly endless series of projects, large and small. Lydia had to collect all types of information about schools, deadlines, tests, and finances. She had to decide where to apply: West Coast, East Coast, somewhere in between?

After several weeks of cluttering up her life with details, Lydia became frustrated with the diddly work and a bit scared of the real work ahead of her. She came into her session complaining. The whole thing was a silly exercise. She wasn't sure she wanted to be a doctor. All doctors were pompous, arrogant, and greedy. No sensible person would want to socialize with stuffy people who just talked shop and stocks. Was it really worth all the effort she was going through? This was the first critical point in Lydia's commitment process. Was she going to continue or was she going to stop? It was her decision. She decided to continue.

After several more weeks of work, there was another critical point. In order to apply to medical school, one needs to take the MCAT (Medical College Admissions Test). To maximize her chances of success on the MCAT, Lydia felt she needed to take a special MCAT preparation course. The course was expensive, four hundred dollars. She rationalized that it was too expensive and that she could study on her own. But she knew the bottom line was commitment. Up to now it had been a game, playing around with catalogs and application forms. But now came the real crunch. Was she going to put her money where her mouth was? After some agonizing, she decided she would take the course.

The application process continued with stops and starts, doubts and pauses. Despite all her fears, Lydia completed the application process. It did wonders for her. Lydia felt much better about her ability to take action, she followed through in ways that she would have never believed, and it boosted her self-esteem to tell people she was applying to medical school. Friends, who had been encouraging her to apply, were delighted, helpful, and supportive.

In the process of applying, Lydia got useful feedback. She did very well on the MCAT. She received superb recommendations. She had interviews at top medical schools. She was dumbfounded.

When she was accepted to medical school, there was yet another critical period of decision. Did she want to go? Could she do it? Why not be a nurse instead? What would it mean to her life? How would it affect her social life? Lydia had reached another stage of the commitment process. She struggled with her decision and decided to go to medical school.

Lydia's story of commitment is more dramatic than most. Medicine is more difficult and requires a higher level of commitment than many occupations. All the more, Lydia's story illustrates the value of limited commitment. We don't need to take a do-or-die stand before we start. We can begin and see what happens.

STRUCTURE

Some cooks take a complicated three-page recipe from a French cookbook and come out with something wonderful. Other cooks open the refrigerator door, grab a handful of this and a dash of that, and come out with something wonderful. There are different ways of doing things. In some cases, there is method to the madness, while in others there is madness to the method. When we get stuck, there is too much madness to the method.

It's hard to make things up as we go along when we are having trouble moving. It's much easier to get cooking when we have a recipe that tells us exactly which ingredients to use and how to mix them all up. We need structure, fine-tuned organization. The more we feel stuck, the more structure we need.

The benefits of structure in terms of effectiveness, efficiency, stress management, and personal satisfaction are enormous. By imposing structure we do the following.

- Give direction: Knowing where to focus and what to ignore keeps us from being distracted by irrelevant matters. This makes us more effective and efficient, gives us a sense of control, and prevents or relieves anxiety.
- Define the task: The more clearly defined the tasks, the more likely we are to begin, persist, and complete them. Conversely, the fuzzier the tasks, the more likely we are to procrastinate or to avoid them entirely. And, the clearer the tasks, the easier it is to evaluate progress and to trouble shoot.
- Define end points: The points at which we say "Done." These are cues for letting ourselves off the hook and rewarding ourselves for our accomplishments. Without clearly defined end points, we never feel finished. We walk around with the tension of incomplete work hanging over our head and we are deprived of the satisfactions of achievement.

People who get stuck have a temporary or chronic difficulty creating structure. Some are obviously disorganized. They don't know where to start. They don't have a plan. They tackle tasks in random order. They work in stops and starts. Others appear to be more methodical. They have a plan. They have lists and charts and sharpened pencils. Yet they don't get things done either. Invariably, upon closer inspection, they are poorly organized: The plans aren't sufficiently well thought out or detailed.

Poor organization is caused by lack of action skills. Those who get stuck usually have some weaknesses in the areas of setting goals, planning, decision making, or stress management. These deficits can lead to haphazard activity, confusion, and anxiety.

We can get caught in a vicious cycle. For want of certain skills, we don't create enough structure. The lack of organization contributes to diminished effectiveness, which in turn contributes to self-doubt and anxiety. These further inhibit the creation of structure and perpetuate the cycle.

A stress symptom that indicates the need for more structure is the experience of being overwhelmed—a common phenomenon in the lives of contemporary women, where the conflicting demands of multiple roles can make one's head spin. When we feel overwhelmed, we think we have too much to handle. Sometimes this is the case. But often we could handle more tasks if we structured them more effectively.

One of the secrets of organizing ourselves is to work around anxiety and other internal resistance to action. Those of us who get stuck don't do this well. Often we recognize our liabilities but ignore them in our planning. We make plans that appear realistic, but they haven't taken our shortcomings into account. When we don't build in ways for managing our liabilities, we trip over them repeatedly, feeling more helpless with each rerun.

This is hardly surprising. If we plan at all, most of us follow rules of efficient behavior such as "first things first." But this type of logic doesn't work well when we are nervous. Important activities create more anxiety than less significant ones. When we are too anxious, we are less alert. Our thoughts may be confused or blocked. Under these circumstances, seemingly reasonable plans may be impossible to implement.

Chapter 8 demonstrates how to structure action so that we can manage our liabilities while working toward our goals. Success with the latter depends on success with the former.

ACCOUNTABILITY

Other people are important characters in our tale of achievement. We strive for them as well as for ourselves. It's our sense of responsibility to others that makes us get up on those mornings when we would prefer to stay in bed.

When we feel stuck, it's important to find someone to report to. We need a person who knows our plans and expects us to follow through on them. We need someone who can judge whether or not we have met our goals and who cares whether or not we do.

In the normal course of events, friends and family don't serve this function. Although they may support our efforts, ordinarily we don't give them detailed progress reports at regular scheduled times. However, this type of structure and accountability is needed. Support, by itself, often isn't enough. When we feel stuck, it's enormously useful to check in with someone on a regular basis.

This may sound silly or even childish, but it isn't. It's a powerful incentive to get going. Self-help groups have recognized this for years. More recently, increasing numbers of diet programs work on this principle, asking dieters to call in their calories or to weigh in on a daily basis. Courses serve a similar function. Several aspiring writers have said that they take courses in order to feel compelled to write. When left to their own devices, they can't count on themselves to keep their typewriters humming.

In counseling, I ask clients to bring in their "homework" assignments and show me their charts, applications, or papers. When people commit themselves to supplying tangible evidence of their work, it makes it more difficult for them to avoid their tasks or to slither away unnoticed if they do. Clients have told me repeatedly, "I wouldn't have done this if it weren't for our session," "Knowing we were going to meet is what got me going," "I couldn't bear the thought of facing you without having done it."

When we make ourselves accountable to another, a private commitment becomes an interpersonal one. This changes the consequences. Breaking promises to ourselves may have little effect. We respond to such broken promises by reproaching ourselves, rationalizing, or forgetting. When we are stuck, we do this so often that self-reproach and rationalization become so habitual that we hardly pay attention to them.

The consequences of breaking a commitment to another person can be serious. We risk disappointment or disapproval. On the positive side, if we come through, we have the opportunity to win approval and respect, and these can be strong incentives for action.

Some are concerned that this type of accountability serves as a crutch. Not at all. Accountability doesn't create dependency any more than training wheels do. We use accountability as a temporary aid to help develop the habits and the skills needed to initiate and complete action. Only when the dependency is prolonged unnecessarily does it become crippling.

Although accountability is important to both men and women, it may be particularly useful for women. Relationships are the traditional domain for women. Working with and doing for others is basic to our psychology. Some psychologists have even argued that achievement in women is motivated by affiliation needs, while achievement in men is motivated by achievement needs. While this is debatable, it makes sense to capitalize on our ties with others to help us get going.

Striving to achieve can be a lonely pursuit. One young writer said, "At some point, I need to hear from my editor because I need to know that there is someone out there." Becoming accountable to someone else is a way of making achievement feel more like a collaborative effort, less lonely, and more satisfying.

We can become accountable to anyone who likes us

and supports our project: a friend, a family member, or a group that we can check in with regularly with progress reports. We need to know that every week Ann or Tom or the study group is expecting to hear about our accomplishments. We can even go one step further and make contracts. More will be said about these later.

We have to ask our friends to work with us. Collaboration won't happen by itself. Working in teams is a good idea. You plan your job hunt with Jane and Jane plans her strategy for becoming more assertive with you, and you check in regularly with each other to exchange progress reports. All sorts of arrangements can be made once the need for accountability is appreciated.

PRACTICE

The idea of practice reminds us of days when we were forced to sit at the piano when we wanted to be out playing with friends. It stirs up memories of teachers who spouted homilies such as "practice makes perfect" while making seemingly unreasonable demands for perfection. The lesson many of us learned is that practice isn't fun. At worst it's unpleasant; at best, boring. After all, who wants to do the same thing over and over again?

But it's repetition that creates behavior patterns. Habits are established and broken through the process of repeated action. Each rerun makes an imprint on the brain and establishes connections that make the behavior easier to execute the next time around.

It's practice, however, only when we do something repeatedly over a relatively narrow span of time. Attempting self-assertion seven times a year isn't practicing; attempting it seven times a week is. If the length of time between trials is too long, we lose the benefit of the previous experience; we forget too much and each attempt feels like the first try.

Repetition isn't always enough. Learning certain skills requires feedback from other people. Good feedback is valuable because it helps us improve and get the most out of practicing. The best type of feedback tells us what we did well, what needs improvement, and how to improve. It's the good news and the bad news.

No one likes the bad news. Even tactfully phrased constructive criticism can sting. Nevertheless, in the long run, it is a blessing. In helping us separate the wheat from the chaff and in suggesting ideas for improvement, constructive criticism points the way to success.

One of the fringe benefits of practice is that it can help to desensitize irrational fears. Each repetition provides additional evidence that fears are unrealistic. The first time we make a sales pitch or assert ourselves in a new way, our knees may shake. The second time, they shake a bit less. By the tenth time, we have forgotten what made us nervous, and by the hundredth, we can do it in our sleep.

Although most of us give lip service to the value of practice, many of us don't really believe it. We imagine that we should be able to do things right the first time. When we don't live up to that expectation, we are distressed and disappointed. This type of perfectionistic thinking is deadly. Unless we truly understand the need for practice we set ourselves up for unnecessary frustration and feelings of failure. If we appreciate the need for practice, we feel less helpless when confronted with mistakes. Instead of lamenting "I will never be able to get this right," we can be more optimistic: "I need more practice. Rome wasn't built in a day."

It's clear that learning some skills demands practice. Playing the piano or skiing are obvious examples. What is less apparent is that a great deal of our behavior consists of habits that are learned through repeated action. Some people take the attitude that you "have it" or you don't. While it's true that some individuals are born with innate talents, most things involve skills that can be learned by anyone.

Women and men are urged to develop different types of behavior patterns. In order to conform to the male code, men are pressured to acquire the skills needed for many kinds of achievement. And they are given the opportunity to practice these skills. Women, on the other hand, don't have the same opportunities. The Junior League doesn't play the same game as the Major League. Most women have had fewer chances to practice pitching. When we join the Major Leagues we have to make up for lost time. We need to figure out the game and keep at it. Our task is to practice mastering the skills of the game and managing our liabilities.

PROGRESS

We already know that success doesn't spring full-blown into our lives, it comes about in stages. A part of this process involves judging how well we are succeeding in meeting our goals.

It would seem that recognizing progress should be easy. But all too often it isn't. Frequently we dismiss or discount small changes. In some cases, all-or-nothing thinking makes us see anything short of total success as failure. We also fail to appreciate progress because we don't understand the path it takes.

Progress begins with the first step, the first phone call, the first sentence, the first application. For people who feel stuck, beginnings are difficult because they are the initial confrontation with both internal psychological resistance and external reality. Overcoming this first hurdle is progress.

Getting through the first several steps often brings on a "high," a sense of excitement and enthusiasm. Even small steps can generate optimism, and once energized, we take more steps. If we have a reasonable amount of success, we can go a long way.

When we feel high, goals seem just within reach. All we need do is continue. But eventually we all run into obstacles: we don't get the role we auditioned for, our short story gets rejected by a magazine, a phone call doesn't get returned. With these inevitable setbacks, we develop greater appreciation for the difficulty or complexity of our tasks. We hit plateaus. We get tired. We get cranky. We want out.

At this point, we shouldn't take our marbles and go home. This is the place to step back and analyze, to figure out what is working and what isn't. With some trial and error, we solve the problems. We feel good again and move on to more success. Then we run into new obstacles. We hit new plateaus. We feel miserable. Once more we solve the problems and continue. And so on and on.

Progress doesn't march forth in a straight line. It's like a dance: two steps forward, one step back; two forward, one back. Knowing the pattern makes it easier to judge progress more realistically. Setbacks are easier to take when we are prepared for them. Forewarned is forearmed.

Sometimes it seems as if nothing is changing. Don't despair. It only *feels* like we are back at square one. In fact, we are playing square one in a new game in an advanced league. Because progress occurs in small steps and change is gradual, we have lost sight of how far we have come.

SUPPORT

We all need warmth and caring to feel good about ourselves. When we feel stuck and our morale is low, we are in particular need of specific types of support: permission and encouragement.

In order to strive, we need to believe that our goals are acceptable. But since achievement hasn't been part of the traditional female role, many women are still uncertain as to whether it is appropriate for them. Contemporary society has responded to this matter with a forked tongue. We have been granted permission to work outside the home, but the battle of how far we can go is still being waged.

Women who get stuck often don't feel entitled to follow their stars. One woman put it this way: "There isn't much support for achievement in my community. Not many women there seem to be trying to make the transition from cooking and knitting to achieving. I feel like I need support for that, and I don't get it anywhere." An aspiring young actress pleaded, "I just want somebody to tell me that it's okay to try." A businesswoman said, "I feel like a puppy trained not to leave the kitchen and go into the living room. So I sit around saying 'Please let me into the living room.' "

Even women with successful careers struggle with these issues. Some career women feel permitted to have only limited aspirations. It's okay for them to have jobs but it isn't okay for them to get rich, have power, or be the best. Until we feel that it's all right to pursue big dreams, we are sitting in the back of the bus.

Ultimately we have to give ourselves permission. But until we find our own, it helps to "borrow" permission from others.

Even when we know our goals and methods are acceptable, we need a cheering section. The most dynamic self-starters need to be spurred on at times. Most people would do so much more if they received some encouragement. This is particularly true of women.

Traditionally women have cheered on men. Conventional roles weren't designed for encouraging women. Females receive less encouragement and more discouragement for achievement throughout school and in the labor force. As a result, we have a greater need for it.

In the best of all possible worlds, we would have a

coach who would grant us permission, teach us how to play, hold us accountable, and encourage us. Since in real life most of us don't have coaches, we have to improvise.

Permission comes from people who tell us through word or example that it's acceptable to pursue our goals. We can get it from role models we find in family, school, work, and social relationships. If we don't have role models readily available, we can find them through networking, an excellent way to make contact with dynamic people. Action-oriented women in any field can give us permission to achieve. Some of us get discouraged because not all successful women qualify for sainthood. It doesn't matter. They demonstrate what can be accomplished, which is all we need from them.

Role models can also be found in the media. Reading about heroes and heroines inspires kids. It works for us big kids as well. Mary Kay Ash, the cosmetics queen, built an empire with God and pink Cadillacs. That doesn't mean we can do the same thing, but it does stretch our perception of what is possible.

We can get encouragement by involving others in our dreams. We can share ideas and plans; initiate discussions about such issues as money, power, and success; ask for opinions, suggestions, and help; look for support groups or form our own; work collaboratively. If we make an active search, we can find what we need.

CHAPTER 7

Focusing

*P*erform every act as if it were the only thing in the world that mattered. . . . It's an old Zen principle—you put your soul and being and life into the act you're performing. In Zen archery your entire being wills the arrow into the bull's-eye with an invisible force. It's not a question of winning, or even caring, it's making everyday acts we all perform important to ourselves."[1]

At the heart of all achievement is concentration, the arrow in the bull's-eye.

When we are stuck, our attention is misplaced: We aren't giving enough thought to our project. Learned helplessness leads our mind elsewhere. We may be distracted, busily engaged in avoidance tactics, preoccupied with fears of failure, or struggling with conflict. Sometimes we get so obsessed with a particular obstacle that we don't see the total picture. Whatever the reason, we aren't concentrating enough on our goals and the means of achieving them.

In order to get going, we have to focus more intensely on the business at hand. In research where participants with low expectations of success were *specifically instructed* to give their complete and undivided attention to the task, their performance improved considerably.[2]

Let me share a similar experience. In my first year of graduate school, the killer course was statistics. Clinical psychology students weren't expected to do well because we were considered "fuzzy-headed" by the supposedly more scientific experimental psychology folk. While I was neither fuzzy-headed nor math phobic, I was intimidated by statistics. When the professor said, "It is obvious that . . . ," which he frequently did, it was never obvious to me. He lost me completely.

Insufficient attention brought me a B− and a C+ on my first two exams. Since C was a failing grade in graduate school, flunking the course became a distinct possibility. I determined never to let that happen! Studying statistics became the main event of my Christmas vacation. Like Seligman's dogs being dragged over the barrier, I read and reread the chapters. At least twenty times. I knew by heart every word, symbol, and number—long before I understood any of it. It might as well have been ancient Greek. But after a while, it started to make sense. Focusing on statistics for a long time allowed my brain to gradually absorb the material. Once enough information was stored in my head, my brain could actively process it. Active processing led to understanding. Then a strange thing happened: Statistics turned into an enjoyable game, a fun puzzle. The real shocker came when I aced the final exam and ranked number two in a class of forty. Everyone, including me, was amazed. One particularly sensitive and gracious male experimental psychology student said, "Hey, Susi, what happened? We were counting on you to hold down the lower end of the curve."

The point is clear: In order to get unstuck we have to focus long enough to get our brain in high gear. We need to pay a great deal of attention to our project and to the behavior patterns that relate to our work. This can be done with the aid of some time-honored devices and some newer behavioral techniques.

FOCUS ON TASKS

If we are staring out of the window instead of doing our homework, the information in our head isn't being put to use. Thoughts about our project are fuzzy and scattered—hardly a frame of mind conducive to action.

The way out of this muddle is to focus on our project in an organized way. Let's begin by looking at the end point of the process—our goal. What do we want to accomplish? What end result do we hope to achieve?

Women's ambitions are as individual as their wardrobes. But work goals typically fall into broad categories. The most common ones are: finding a job, changing a career, starting or expanding a business, applying to school, acquiring or increasing a skill, improving productivity and efficiency, solving a specific work problem, and making more money. Women in corporate settings have aims specific to those environments. These include: being promoted; improving relationships with superiors, peers, and/or subordinates; obtaining resources for their divisions; coping with political crises; and acquiring power.

Identifying a broad category is only a start. A well-defined goal is positive and specific. For example, suppose you want to leave your job because the disorganization of the company is demoralizing. You might be inclined to say,

"I have to get out of this madhouse before I go nuts." But this negative goal only describes what you want to escape. That isn't enough. We need to think in terms of what we are seeking. Instead you might say, "I want to work in a well-run company." This statement directs your attention to what you want; and the more you look at your target, the better your chances of hitting it.

A vague desire is a pipe dream. A clear goal is *specific*. Nailing down the details of *what* and *when* allows us to quickly eliminate dead ends and to focus our attention on more promising prospects. A time frame brings the goal into current reality rather than letting it float out in the wild blue yonder of an uncharted future. Suppose, for example, you come up short at the end of each month. You might say, "I want to make more money." Well, a monthly increase of two dollars would constitute more money, but that's probably not what you have in mind. A more useful formulation of your goal might be, "I want to make 10 percent more in the next six months." This statement spells out exactly what you want and can serve as a guide for action.

Although precise thinking is important, once we begin to take action the specifics may change. Feedback from our activities tells us what works and what doesn't, what feels good and what feels bad. This information may lead us to modify our goal accordingly.

Once we have defined our goal in positive and specific terms, we need to focus on how to tackle it. The easiest way to do this is to make a list. Simply write down everything that needs to be done to accomplish the goal. For example, if you want to apply to graduate school, your list might include such items as:

- sending away for catalogs
- filling out applications
- sending out transcripts

- getting references
- taking entrance exams

When you have doubts about your goals, you can use list making to help gain greater clarity. Ask yourself, "If I were to accomplish ———, what would I need to do?" Walking yourself through this can help to sort out ideas and feelings.

Sometimes our need is to find a specific goal, such as a career direction or a new field. In this case the project consists of gathering enough information to establish a definite career goal. Here the list would consist of strategies for discovering and exploring options. It might include items such as:

- networking
- reading
- taking courses
- attending workshops and seminars
- going on informational interviews
- obtaining career counseling

List making is one of the oldest tricks in the book. It's powerful because it forces us to articulate, assemble, and analyze ideas that have been scattered, vague, and inchoate in our mind. Paradoxically, because it is such a cliché, many of us overlook the obvious and don't do it. Others make lists but don't make them detailed enough to facilitate effective action.

Details

The more we focus, the easier it is to come up with specific items for our list. The more detailed the list, the easier it is to begin, to follow through, and to solve problems. Researchers have found that people who paid attention to details improved their problem-solving ability more than those who didn't.[3]

Let's take an example. In the fifth year of Kim's employment at the marketing department of the ABC publishing company, a corporate shake-up resulted in Kim's reporting to a new superior. The relationship got off to a bad start and went downhill from there. After six months of deteriorating communications, Kim was asked to resign. She felt very bad about herself and found it difficult to look for another job. Since she had savings and severance pay, she didn't feel economic pressure to look for a new position immediately and kept postponing the job hunt.

Kim began pulling herself together by making the following list of what she needed to do:

- write a résumé
- network
- ask people for references
- check out the classifieds
- contact headhunter

Such a list is a start, but it can be broken down into considerably more detail. Let's take just one item, writing the résumé, and break it down into smaller parts:

- review old résumé
- write a detailed description of current job responsibilities
- type up rough draft
- get opinions of the draft
- make revisions
- have résumé typed
- have résumé printed

By the time we have finished such a detailed list we have a clearer picture of what needs to be done, we can estimate the amount of time and energy needed, and we can schedule tasks at our convenience. In short, we have laid the groundwork for a good plan.

A detailed list helps to reveal weaknesses in thinking.

When we can't be specific or can't execute some of the tasks on the list, we have to get more information or rethink our strategies or goals.

This point came home to Muriel, who wanted to expand her small gift shop but couldn't get started. She decided to make two lists: one list of tasks for the next six months and another for the next two years. She easily came up with items for her six-month plan. But when it came to the long-range project, her list was very short. Muriel quickly realized that she needed a great deal more information before she could make a realistic two-year plan. She immediately put "research" at the top of her list.

Under certain circumstances, such as when we have a difficult project or when we feel emotional distress, making a list is particularly important. At these times, a detailed list can:

- help us make the connection between the ends and the means. This reinforces the idea that our actions influence the outcome, and gives us a sense of control.
- bring order and direction to the project, and thereby reduce confusion and anxiety.
- allow us to step back from our thinking and look at it objectively. In particular, it can help us separate the concrete tasks from associated anxieties. For example, as we detail the process of producing a résumé, we can see that the anxiety induced by the résumé has little to do with the actual organizing, writing, and typing. The anxiety comes from thoughts associated with the process, such as doubts about competence.
- bring the goal into sight. Regardless of the length of the list, there is an end to it. Tasks seem less overwhelming when there is a light at the end of the tunnel.

FOCUS ON BEHAVIOR

Looking closely at the thoughts, actions, and feelings that relate to our work is another way to get unstuck. Focusing on our behavior gives us a badly needed sense of control. We are affirming that we can effectively manage ourselves and are taking action that allows us to do so. Often this has the fringe benefit of reducing anxiety.

Concentrating on our behavior brings self-knowledge. Heightened alertness permits us to observe features and details we wouldn't ordinarily notice. For example, a woman who lacked self-confidence began focusing on her feminine discounting habit. After doing this for a week, she reported, "I was surprised at how much I automatically attribute to luck!"

As we gain self-knowledge, the features of our psychological landscape begin to stand out in sharp relief. New patterns emerge. We find chains of behavior with links in predictable sequences. Subtle connections, previously obscured, become apparent. Odd bits of behavior, seemingly random, begin to make sense.

This type of information is essential for planning and implementing strategies for change. As our recognition of patterns and linkages increase, the possibilities for intervening multiply. The more we can predict, the more we can control.

People sometimes say, "I have gained all this understanding, I know why I do what I do, so why don't I act differently?" The reason is simple. Insight, by itself, doesn't change habits. We need immediate awareness, not abstract knowledge, to alter our routines. Insight fosters change only when it helps us to focus on crucial behavior patterns in day-to-day life. Without daily application, gaining insight is like buying a bicycle and never riding it.

How to Focus

When I was a little girl, I was fascinated by automobiles and used to entertain myself on long rides by counting Buicks. Why Buicks? Because the old ones had long chrome rods on the grillwork that reminded me of teeth. Since they were the only cars with "teeth," I could tell them apart from all the others. So, as I rode along, I scanned all the cars on the highway, and when I spotted teeth, I chalked up another Buick.

This is essentially what we do when we focus. Since we can't observe all of our behavior all of the time, any more than I could count all the cars on the road, we pick out one type of behavior and keep a lookout for it as we go through our day. When we spot it, we make a mental note and pay extra close attention to what is going on.

Focusing in a consistent and systematic way is made easier with the use of self-monitoring aids such as diaries.

Much popular attention has been given to diaries from weight watchers. Dieters record their daily food intake to help them control it. The same principle holds for other types of behavior. You choose what you want to focus on— the *target behavior*—and write down its daily occurrence.

In practice, it's very simple. Get a notebook that is easy to write in and carry around. Find something you like; the more comfortable you are with the actual writing, the more likely you are to stay with it.

Record your behavior each time you observe it. Write things down right away or as soon thereafter as possible. Don't let several hours elapse before making your entry.

Be specific. Describe the details of the target behavior, and where possible describe the situation or the circumstances that preceded the behavior and the consequences or the events that followed it.

There are several advantages to keeping records. To begin with, this elevates the process of focusing to the status of a project, giving it more priority and energy. As a result, it's less likely to become another overlooked good intention.

Second, because self-monitoring allows us to observe and record our behavior systematically, it's more accurate. Any dieter can describe the discrepancy between what she "thinks" she eats and what she actually writes down. Not only is it easy to forget, memories can be distorted by wishes and needs. Writing forces us to observe more carefully in order to get the needed details. This in turn makes it easier to develop strategies for change and to evaluate progress.

Third, an accurate and detailed picture can suggest causes and even solutions. Connie's experience is a case in point.

Connie, a twenty-seven-year-old computer programmer, came to counseling complaining of lack of confidence in her work. She had a bad case of the feminine discounting habit. She was completely straight-faced as she suggested that she graduated from college with a degree in math because of her charm and social skill. Only half of her really believed this, but it was enough to undermine her confidence.

This showed in Connie's work. Somewhat unassertive, she seldom spoke up at meetings. She was cooperative to the point of being passive; she accepted what she was told rather than asking any challenging questions. She was afraid of asking questions, challenging or otherwise, out of fear of revealing her basic lack of intelligence. In the class she attended as part of her work, it was more of the same. When the instructor asked a question, she quietly mumbled the answer under her breath, but didn't actually speak up.

For all her insecurities, however, Connie was competent and respected. Most of the time, she was able to keep a lid on her vulnerabilities. Nevertheless, her problem with confidence came to a head when she did poorly on an exam and passed the course by the skin of her teeth. Since course work was a requirement of her job, more than just her ego was at stake. She was afraid that her lack of confidence might jeopardize her career.

Since the acute problem was Connie's anxiety about tests, we looked at that. We already knew something about the anxiety and its consequences. As she put it: "I get clutched on tests. I get nervous, I misread, I misinterpret, I reverse things."

What we didn't know was how this chain of events was set off. Connie agreed to monitor her thoughts before and, to the extent possible, during the next exam. Since she couldn't record all her thoughts, she limited it to only thoughts that could, by any stretch of the imagination, be described as negative.

The results were enlightening. She discovered that prior to and during the exam, she had helpless thoughts combined with unproductive comparisons. Here is a sample:

Before the Exam:

- Shortly before the exam I went to my locker and I didn't believe I could remember the combination to my lock.
- Immediately before the exam I thought: I will never get an A.
- I wondered how much Michael (the class whiz) had studied.

During the Exam (she wrote this down after the test was over):

- I took one look at the problem and said, "I can't do this."
- I wondered, What problem is Michael working on now?
- How can Jeff be finished already? Did he ace it or blow it?

This one monitoring exercise gave Connie a wealth of information. She immediately understood how she was getting in her own way. She was thinking helpless thoughts. And she was distracting herself with irrelevant concerns— what Michael and Jeff were doing didn't matter. The only thing that mattered was doing her best.

Once she identified a cause of the problem, a solution became apparent immediately. Stop the self-defeating thinking: the helpless commentary and the comparison shopping.

Appreciating this, Connie continued to monitor her thoughts and was able to stop herself easily. By the time she took the final exam several weeks later, she made no negative remarks or comparisons. And once she made this dent in her problem, Connie's confidence began to rise. Not everyone can shed bad habits as easily as Connie did, but anyone can learn from the process of self-monitoring.

Connie was able to reduce her self-defeating thinking simply by focusing on it and recording it. In fact, on the very first day of self-monitoring, Connie noted a reduction in the number of her comparisons.

Her experience isn't an isolated case. Psychologists have found that the very act of monitoring behavior, *by itself*, can bring about a change. Since the observed behavior seems to "react" to the observation process, the phenomenon was termed *reactivity*.

The change in the observed behavior isn't random. Monitoring behavior we care about tends to bring about a change in the "right" direction. A considerable amount of research has demonstrated this.[4] Dieters who counted calories reduced their caloric intake. Smokers who monitored their smoking smoked less, and worriers who monitored their worrying worried less. People with nervous habits such as squinting and arm jerking reported fewer twitches when they kept records. On the other hand, when quiet students monitored their class participation, they spoke up more. And when people with phobias (such as fear of animals, or closed or open spaces) self-monitored, they increased their tolerance for the situations that frightened them.

It's fascinating, and how it works isn't fully understood. But the moral of the story is clear: By recording observations of our behavior, we increase our chances of controlling it.

Karen used self-monitoring to control angry feelings in the office. Karen worked in the same office as her former boyfriend, Fred—in fact, their desks were right next to each other. As long as they were dating, this arrangement was cozy. But once they broke up, it turned into a horror show. To begin with, Karen could overhear Fred's amorous chats with his newest flame. Even worse was Fred's unpleasant habit of putting Karen down. Although they were peers, Fred had a way of treating Karen like his assistant in the presence of their boss. It drove her wild. These go-arounds could put Karen in a stew for hours and a really nasty one could ruin her entire day. One time, she lost her temper and ended up looking foolish in the eyes of her superior. To add insult to injury, Fred seemed to love every minute of it.

Realizing the uproar was undermining her confidence and effectiveness, Karen felt an urgent need to do something about it. She agreed to monitor the episodes in her diary. Immediately after an irritating encounter with Fred, Karen wrote up the incident in blow-by-blow detail. Fred did . . . , Karen did . . . , Fred did . . . , etc.

Karen found that by doing this she was able to reduce her distress considerably. By focusing and writing she was able to distance herself and to interrupt the downward spiral that had previously resulted in her getting angrier and angrier. Karen short-circuited the entire sequence of misery-inducing thoughts through self-monitoring.

Anticipating instant success is unrealistic and I usually caution people against it. However, spontaneous problem solving occurs frequently enough to make it worth mentioning. It happens when we are able to modify what we are thinking or doing as soon as we recognize the problem. If we hadn't focused, we wouldn't have seen the difficulty. But having spotted the troublemaker, we can do something about it immediately.

Helen, who was focusing on her feminine discounting habit, gave the following example:

> It was a rainy day and my car, which sometimes gets temperamental in wet weather, wouldn't start. I desperately needed it to start because I was in the midst of moving to a new apartment. I eventually got it started by using a wire drier. Later I told my boyfriend the story and found myself remarking on how *lucky* I was. Then suddenly I thought of myself as being able to handle a car. I usually think of myself as having no knowledge of cars, but that's not true. I do know something.

Helen made an immediate adjustment in her self-image. Of course, one incident won't overhaul a person's self-image. But many experiences, over a period of time, will make a difference. By focusing, we provide ourselves with opportunities to challenge our negative self-image. In the course of doing this, we can develop a more accurate picture of ourselves and gain self-confidence.

Versatility

All behavior that can be observed and clearly defined can be recorded. People use diaries to focus in a variety of situations.

When monitoring unassertive behavior, we can take a general or a specific approach. When we aren't sure where our difficulties lie, we can take a general survey. In the course of one or two weeks we can observe and record all the situations in which we felt unassertive and/or uncomfortable. Discomfort isn't always an indication of lack of assertion, but often it is a helpful clue. Sometimes we recognize our unassertiveness only after the fact; even focusing on what we wish we'd said or done can teach us something.

Most of us do have areas of strength in which self-assertion comes easily, along with areas of vulnerability in which it is difficult. Some can ask for things but can't say no. Others can talk positively about themselves but can't confront. Still others can speak to a large group of strangers but not to a small group of colleagues. It's individual. The point of a general survey is to sort this out.

Alternatively, when we already know our trouble spots, we can focus specifically on them. We pick a particular type of assertion and monitor it as we go through the week. Consider Lucy, a college instructor and part-time consultant, who had a hard time asking for things. It was difficult for her to set fees and demand payment for her consulting work. More subtly, her difficulty crept into her daily life in many small ways that added up to inefficiency and ineffectiveness. In particular, she had trouble asking for things on the telephone. As a result, she often avoided and postponed phone calls, which hurt her business.

She decided to focus on assertion involving asking for things. She monitored both when she did ask and when she wanted to but didn't. Here is a record of her first week:

Monday, March 14:
Called office for details about professor exchange program. Felt momentary suspense while ringing. Got hold of the secretary, who will send me information.

Tuesday, March 15:
Asked friend if I could borrow her typist for some rush work. No problem.

Wednesday, March 16:
Called Brian Rogers about contract he said he would send
me. Had put it off for a week. I was pleased to find he was
out of town. Left message.

Did not do:
Call proposed guest speaker for my class. Should have
called this week. Now I will have to postpone that talk and
rearrange curriculum.

Call to set up appointment with government agency to
discuss possible project.

Ask for tinfoil for meat scraps for dog at the wedding
where other people at the table did.

Didn't state preference about a movie, when I really
preferred one. Said it didn't matter.

In assessing this assortment of professional and personal experiences, Lucy concluded that monitoring had
helped her pay attention to some calls and requests. However, she felt that she needed to do additional work with
the problem.

Self-monitoring, by itself, will help assertion problems
when the inertia of old habits is the primary culprit. In this
type of situation, focusing is a way of giving ourselves a
reminder to do what we know we can do. But when strong
anxiety or lack of skill is involved, additional tactics are
needed.

Focusing on how we spend our time is another way of
gaining control over our behavior. This is particularly useful
when we are doing too little and/or are inefficient in our
activities. We can monitor time in a number of different
ways, each serving a somewhat different purpose.

Leslie is a twenty-two-year-old woman who got stuck
in her job hunt after graduating from college. She has a
high level of intelligence and a low level of persistence.
When she isn't immediately successful, she concludes that

the situation is hopeless and gives up. As a result, after several months of sporadic job hunting, she stopped looking. Living at home with generous parents enabled Leslie to survive unemployment with relatively little economic hardship.

But despite her creature comforts, Leslie felt ill at ease with her life-style. Sleeping away days and partying away nights began to be demoralizing. She wanted to work but couldn't get herself back in gear.

With some reservations, she agreed to keep a diary of how she spent her time. She didn't look forward to the prospect of doing it because she wasn't eager to confront how she was living. Nevertheless, she monitored her time in hour intervals. Here is a sample of her first day:

Tuesday, February 3:
12 P.M.—got up, showered, washed and dried hair, dressed
1—ate, chatted with mother
2—walked into shopping center, did errand, window-shopped, went home
3:30—read newspaper, watched television
4—ditto
5—ditto, called friend, made plans for the evening
6—helped mother prepare dinner, ate
7—went over to Jeannie's house
8—went to club with Jeannie and roommate
9—had some drinks, talked with guys
10—ditto
11—Jeannie met a guy; I got bored, went home
12 A.M.—watched television
12:30—bed

Keeping track of her time this way and focusing on how little she was accomplishing embarrassed Leslie into action. After a week of keeping her diary, she resumed her job hunt. That brought up other issues, but she had begun to move.

Eileen had another type of problem with time. She wasn't using it efficiently and this was adding to her problems. A graduate student with strong fears of failure, Eileen often had difficulty concentrating on her studies. After a relatively short time, her mind would wander and then her body would follow suit. If she wasn't careful, she would wind up in the kitchen studying potato chips instead of finance.

Although she also monitored time, Eileen focused on how much she actually studied. She noted when she started studying, and each time she started daydreaming she recorded that she had stopped studying. Here is a sample of her record.

Thursday, November 17:

Started	Stopped
8 P.M.	8:20
8:23	9:10
9:30	10:15
10:30	11:02
11:03	11:45

Eileen felt that monitoring her study time helped her pay more attention to her work. By forcing herself to notice what she was doing, she was able to pull herself back into reality much sooner than in the past. She continued monitoring and found that her concentration improved.

Joyce hated making decisions. She went food shopping once a month in a small, overpriced grocery to avoid the nightmare of choosing among fifty varieties of cheese and thirty brands of crackers at the supermarket.

Despite this, she was eager for a challenging job and was thrilled to be offered the position of business manager in a large mental health center. Once she started working, she quickly realized why she was so well paid. Funds were being cut and her job was one big headache. She had to make hundreds of decisions in a constantly changing scene. She was confronted with choices that ran the gamut from selecting stationery to determining salaries. And all this in an agency bubbling over with professional rivalry and antagonism.

She described her feelings this way: "I was never in a position before where the decisions were important. Now I have big decisions and no clear guidelines. It makes me very nervous. I remember the wrong decisions, and the iffy ones, but I forget the right ones. The worst thing, though, is that many decisions just seem to keep hanging in midair, never getting settled."

In order to get a handle on her decision making, Joyce began keeping a diary in which she recorded the following:

- date
- the situation and the issues to be decided
- alternatives
- advantage and disadvantage of each alternative
- the rationale for her choice

For example, a question arose because the mental health center was moving to smaller quarters. The new occupants of the old quarters offered to buy certain pieces of furniture. The decision was whether or not to sell the furniture. Joyce recorded the following:

August 3, 1989:

Decision: Sell furniture or not?
Advantages of Selling:
1. Extra money available immediately.
2. Offered price was good.
3. Easy, no effort involved in finding a buyer.

Disadvantages:

1. Uncertain about whether these pieces of furniture would be needed in new offices; that would depend on other decisions to be made in the future.

2. If they ended up selling needed furniture, they would have to buy new furniture at higher prices.

Advantages of Not Selling:

1. Furniture will be available for new quarters at no further cost.

Disadvantages:

1. Lose available buyer. Will have to invest time and energy in selling furniture later.

2. May not get as good a price.

Decision and Rationale:

Decided not to sell. The convenience and profit weren't worth the risk involved.

Almost immediately after Joyce began keeping notes, she felt more in control. For her, keeping a diary was an affirmation of her right to make decisions. And, of course, she felt more organized. Instead of having many decisions floating around in her brain, creating additional tension as she tried to keep track of them, Joyce packaged them neatly in one place.

In reviewing her diary, Joyce found that despite her impressions to the contrary, decisions did get made. She even made some good ones. When she did make mistakes, her reasoning—given the information available at the time—made sense. Collecting data that demonstrated her logic was sound, even when decisions backfired, made Joyce feel more secure. Over a period of months, she stopped condemning her "terrible judgment" and her confidence increased.

Resistance

People sometimes say things like "I don't like to keep records." Or "It's too much bother." Or "I am not good at that." Or sometimes they agree to do it and don't follow through. In other words, they resist the idea of focusing and/or collecting data.

There are two typical reasons for this resistance. The first is nuisance: We don't want to be bothered doing extra work. The second is avoidance: We prefer to do the ostrich routine and ignore the reality of our behavior. The two are often confused. What passes for laziness is really unacknowledged avoidance.

It's possible to focus without keeping records and to learn something from the experience. However, it's unlikely that most people will continue focusing long or accurately enough. People who self-monitor have a much better chance of changing their behavior than those who don't.

With respect to avoidance, it's extremely difficult to change our behavior if we aren't prepared to confront it. Changing habits requires awareness of our behavior when we are engaging in it. It's the price of admission.

WHEN FOCUS ISN'T ENOUGH

By focusing on tasks and on behavior patterns with the aid of lists and diaries, we can often give ourselves enough of a push to start moving. By actively working to keep our eye on the ball, we can get hold of it and start running with it. Sometimes that's all it takes. Once in motion, we build up sufficient momentum to keep going.

Other times, things don't work out so neatly. For those situations we need something more. In the next chapters, we will look at strategies and techniques designed to keep the ball in play.

CHAPTER 8

Tackling Tasks

You can't get there from here" is the punch line of a classic comic routine. Although it's not so funny in real life, that's exactly how we feel when we are stuck. We may start walking but we don't believe we're going to get anywhere. Well, we *can* get there from here. The trick is to get directions and make a map or, to be more precise, a plan.

We have already begun working on the plan by making a list. Now we must elaborate. We need to organize the projects into steps, arrange these steps in a workable sequence, and schedule them into our daily life. To these basic ingredients, we add strategies designed to make tackling tasks easier and less anxiety provoking. Once this plan is mapped out, we are ready to take the show on the road.

STEPS

The thought of writing a book intimidates many people. Of course it is hard work. However, it's much less awe-inspiring when you consider that you don't actually write a book. What you "write" are sentences. The sentences become paragraphs and the paragraphs become sections and the sections become chapters. Eventually, God willing, the chapters become a book.

The same logic applies to all we do. Once we have formulated our goal and decided how to achieve it, we must break tasks up into small, manageable steps and create "mini" goals that we tackle one at a time. Bit by bit, from milepost to milepost, we make our way toward the finish line.

The secret of reaching our destination is making our steps *small enough* so that we can accomplish our goals with minimal strain and pain.

The most common mistake is taking too big a step. We bite off more than we can possibly chew. Unfortunately, we imagine we have set reasonable goals. When we don't achieve them, we blame our incompetence and get discouraged. After a few rounds of this we feel stuck.

Sometimes taking too big a bite is simply inexperience. We don't appreciate the amount of work, time, or energy a particular task will demand. Other times we feel guilty because we think we are taking things too easy. We think of ourselves as lazy or unmotivated.

Most troublesome, though, is getting confused by "shoulds." We take too-large steps because we base plans on what we imagine we "should be able to do" rather than on what we actually can do.

This comes up repeatedly for those of us who are anxious or phobic. We plan in terms of how we would act if we weren't afraid. By failing to take our discomfort into account, we end up trying to take giant steps, imagining they're reasonable ones. For example, we might assume that we should be able to finish all the graduate school applications in one week. Well, perhaps in the best of all possible worlds completing applications wouldn't be a giant step. But when we have strong fears of failure, *it is* a giant step. If we don't treat it as such, we are likely to fall flat on our faces or, frozen with fear, do nothing.

Linda is a twenty-seven-year-old mental health worker in a state hospital. Having become interested in counseling, she sent away for applications to social work programs. The applications started coming in. They piled up on her bookshelf but she couldn't bring herself to fill them out. Days passed. Every time Linda thought about the applications, she got nervous and suddenly remembered other things, like the laundry, that needed attention.

I suggested that Linda break down the task into extremely small steps. The first was to write her name on all the forms. She laughed. It was such an absurdly small step it could hardly be taken seriously. But she did it. Once she had written down her name, it wasn't so difficult to fill in her address and telephone number. Having gotten that far, filling out the rest of the factual material was relatively painless. Needless to say, writing essays on the joys of becoming a social worker was much harder. However, by the time the rest of the application form had been completed, she felt more optimistic about her ability to follow through.

People always laugh when they hear this example— but they always get the point. When we feel stuck, we have to break down the tasks into steps that are small enough so that we can *do something*.

The more difficult the task, the greater our anxiety or

inclination to avoid, the smaller our steps. It's always better to err on the side of moving too slowly. No step is too small.

By making projects more manageable and less overwhelming, small steps reduce anxiety and make it easier to get started. However, there are other benefits as well. Little tasks are easier and increase our chances of success. And, in the event that we fall, we will take only a small spill and our recovery will be speedy.

Since smaller steps take less time to complete, we can get the satisfaction of finishing them sooner. Or, to put it another way, we don't have to wait until a big chunk of work is done in order to feel good about ourselves. We can experience success early and often. This sense of accomplishment is particularly important because it is incentive to continue.

Small steps also allow us to schedule more efficiently. They can be squeezed into whatever period of time may be available. For example, the owner of a sewing shop sold fancy pillows that she made in her spare time. Making an entire pillow took several hours and she had few such large blocks of time available. But once she broke the project into steps—cutting out a pattern, sewing four seams, sewing in the zipper, stuffing it—she found she was able to fit the steps in at odd moments and could make many more pillows.

With small steps we can multiply the hours of the day and the successes we achieve in them.

Sequence: Down the Path of Least Resistance

When we bake a cake, the order in which we mix our ingredients is crucial. On the other hand, when we prepare a salad, it doesn't matter whether we slice the cucumbers before or after the tomatoes. When there is a preordained sequence to our work, we have to respect it. But in most projects there is some leeway and we have the freedom to arrange some of the steps according to our personal preference.

When we are stuck, there is a guiding principle for organizing our steps. It's expressed well in the words of an old love song: "Make it easy on yourself."

This may seem to run counter to common sense and to the values of the work ethic, but it's an effective strategy. Under different circumstances, we might be more concerned with priorities or efficiency. But when it's hard to get going, the best road is the path of least resistance.

A woman in middle management began a job hunt by checking out the classifieds. She didn't really expect to find a position through the newspaper, but it was a reasonable and *easy* first step. Another woman, one who had been out of the job market for several years due to illness and drug abuse, could barely get herself to look at the newspaper. Her first step was simply to skim one page of the want ads. She gradually worked up to skimming the entire section. After several weeks she took her next major step: circling potential leads. A third woman, a self-employed consultant, felt anxious about going out and hustling more badly needed business. She began her marketing campaign by plowing through a backlog of paperwork. Finishing that wouldn't bring her new clients but it was a gentle way of gearing up for the big push.

We find our first steps by looking at our list of tasks and asking ourselves questions such as these:

- What am I able to do right now?
- What is the easiest thing for me to do?
- What is the fastest?
- What is the most fun?
- What is the least intimidating?

The critical thing is to find a starting point. Taking action helps to restore a perception of control and to lessen the sense of helplessness. The feeling of success generated by even a seemingly trivial accomplishment can inspire optimism and the desire to carry on. Using this logic, we plan the next steps. Of the remaining tasks, which one is the most comfortable? Which one after that?

What is easy or difficult varies enormously from person to person. For some, it's technically difficult work, while for others, it's a matter of psychological stress. Often it's some unbeatable combination of both. Some people panic when they see numbers, others when they have to write a sentence of more than five words. The person who whizzes through an interview may freeze on an exam. Another would rather scrub floors with a toothbrush than make a phone call. It's highly individual. Our arrangement of steps depends on what feels good *to us*.

In theory, the entire game plan should be mapped out in advance, but in practice, this doesn't always work. Sometimes we don't have enough information at the beginning of a venture; sometimes we feel too overwhelmed or anxious to think clearly about the more difficult steps. That's all right. All we need at the beginning is an overview to establish an overall sequence of steps. Once we have that, we need a detailed program of action for the first several steps. Having completed those, we can then begin to fine-tune or reevaluate the next several moves. Once we get a few tasks out of the way, two things happen: We feel more confidence and the work pile has become smaller. As a result, the entire project is easier to tackle.

Scheduling

It's easy to forget. It's easy to be busy. It's easy to be tired. Unless we deliberately schedule time for our project, our "soup" may evaporate on the back burner while we are attending to the specialty of the house.

There are several tips for scheduling that are particularly useful when feeling stuck.

Double Time. Not scheduling enough time is a common mistake. When we are anxious, we often need more time than usual because anxiety can reduce efficiency. To ensure enough time, it's helpful to use the following rule of thumb: Make a conservative estimate of the time needed and double it. This will allow for anxiety, underestimates, interruptions, and unanticipated crises and will help reduce stress-provoking time crunches.

Prime Time. Whenever possible, it's best to match a difficult and/or stressful activity with what time management consultant Alan Lakein calls *prime time*.[1] This is the time of day when we have the most energy, can concentrate the best, and get the most accomplished. Planning tough jobs for low-energy periods may create unnecessary stress and undermine effectiveness. There isn't much point to burning the midnight oil if we can't keep our eyes open after 10:00 P.M.

Tea Time. When a task needs to be done routinely, setting aside the same time each day is a great help. For example, if you need to study regularly, you might schedule the hours from 8:00 P.M. to 10:00 P.M. on a daily basis. This eliminates the stress and bother of decision making and encourages the establishment of habits, both of which save energy and increase efficiency.

Time management is a relatively new idea for many women. We haven't learned to value our time and to treat it as an asset. Accustomed to being at the beck and call of others, we aren't used to thinking of our time as a commodity that we can or should control. As a result, we often lack skills in time management and don't even realize it. Poor time management can create misery. It can cause us to feel overwhelmed, reduce our efficiency, and cut down our free time. The problems are multiplied when our distress is misdiagnosed. If we don't appreciate that poor time management is contributing to our difficulties, it's a setup for attributing them to lack of ability. When this happens, the time management problem gets overlooked—and remains unresolved—as we get caught up in a sense of helplessness about our ability to manage our lives.

Laura, a thirty-one-year-old law student, had a longstanding problem with fear of failure—and its sidekick, procrastination. She had been a very bright child who, despite poor work habits, received A's with little effort. Her casual approach to school continued through college, where she got fairly decent grades by cramming at the twelfth hour.

Although her grades were good enough to get her into law school, her study habits weren't adequate to ensure her success. Last-minute cramming wouldn't work in law school and she knew it. She tried to study regularly but ran into difficulty. Her inability to control her schoolwork made her feel incompetent and lowered her self-esteem.

A major cause of Laura's problem was that she had fallen into an unsatisfying routine. She came home at five o'clock, took a shower, cooked dinner, ate, and cleaned up. At eight, she started studying. By nine she was restless and began wandering around her apartment. Invariably she stopped in the kitchen for a snack and then settled down in front of the television. At ten-thirty, she returned to her books and continued working until twelve-thirty. By then her anxiety had worn off and she could study efficiently.

Inadvertently, Laura established a routine that made life needlessly unpleasant for her. She scheduled an extremely long block of study time, from eight to twelve-thirty; and she created a conflict for herself by planning to study during her favorite television program.

Once she recognized this, Laura was able to solve her problem by changing her schedule. When she came home she gave herself half an hour to unwind. From five-thirty to eight she studied. Then she showered, ate, cleaned up, and watched television. At ten-thirty she resumed studying until twelve-thirty. By adjusting her routine to better satisfy her personal needs, Laura was able to increase her studying.

Managing time well is a matter of self-knowledge, time management know-how, and a bit of trial and error. It's a very individual matter. The best way is what *works for you*.

ADDITIONAL STRATEGIES AND TECHNIQUES

The basic strategy—breaking the project into small steps, arranging them in a comfortable sequence, and scheduling them—can be deceptive. It's simple in that it's uncomplicated and easy to understand. But it doesn't work unless it's implemented. Often it requires trial and error and practice before getting the knack of it. Sometimes additional tactics are needed to overcome inner resistance.

Warm-ups

Some of us, particularly those who fear failure, have difficulty getting started. We procrastinate, waste time, and then feel bad about ourselves for doing so.

One way to handle this is to use warm-ups. In the same way dancers and athletes do preliminary exercises to prepare their bodies for major exertion, we can psyche ourselves up for hard work. Instead of tackling the task head-on, we can ease ourselves into it by starting with some activity that helps us shift gears. For example, one woman warmed up for studying by doing crossword puzzles. The particular activity is a matter of personal preference; whatever works will do.

In writing this book, I used two very common strategies. When my head was full of ideas and I wasn't sure where to start, I warmed up by straightening up. I cleaned my desk, sorted papers, and rearranged files and books. At other times, when I needed to stimulate my thinking, I skimmed books and articles and typed up notes. Both activities helped to get me going.

Warm-ups can be used for interpersonal situations as well. Psychologist Charles Garfield found that a common characteristic of high achievers was the habit of mentally rehearsing key situations.[2] Before entering high-level conferences, important interviews, or significant sales meetings, peak performers concentrated on visualizing the details of the process and desired outcomes, and etched successful actions in their brains.

We can do the same. Prior to an important phone call or meeting, we can focus on it. We can review the issues, the cast of characters and their opinions, the different turns the discussion might take, and our role in the drama. In some instances, it's even useful to write out a script and practice our lines. For example, when asking for a raise in salary, it can be helpful to write out the reasons for the request, the anticipated responses, and the counterarguments to unenthusiastic replies.

The Self-Management Chart

This is a simple device designed to aid in maintaining focus on daily tasks. Its purpose is to prevent us from forgetting or ignoring essential tasks and to help us be accountable to ourselves.

At the beginning of each week, make up a chart. Use the rows for the days of the week, and columns for the activities you wish to focus on (or vice versa). At the end of each day, check off all the tasks you worked on that day. One activity that belongs on every chart is *looking at the chart*. Always reserve the first column (or row) for that.

Judy, a department store buyer, needed to call friends and colleagues to inform them that she was looking for a new position. She felt uncomfortable about making these calls, imagining that the desire for a career change indicated some failure on her part, and found herself postponing or forgetting them in the course of her busy work day. She used a self-management chart to help her pay more attention to her networking activities. Here's what her chart looked like for the first week:

Self-Management Chart #1

	Check Chart	Call Contacts
Monday	X	
Tuesday	X	
Wednesday	X	
Thursday	X	X
Friday	X	X

Since this week Judy avoided making calls until Thursday, she checked off Thursday and Friday and left the other three days blank. Although she didn't call every day, she did look at her chart every day and therefore checked off the first column daily.

A nursing student was having difficulty managing her schoolwork and used the chart to help her with her studies. It looked like this:

Self-Management Chart #2

	M	T	W	T	F	S	S
Check Chart	X	X	X	X	X	X	X
Study Pharmacology				X	X		
Work on Health Care Plans	X	X	X		X		
Psychology Paper	X	X	X	X	X		

She organized her chart differently, but the idea is the same. She divided her studying into several projects and checked off whenever she worked on one of them. By doing this, she saw where she was investing her energy and what she was avoiding. Although she had studied, she hadn't done enough pharmacology, and the chart helped her confront that.

In a way, the "check chart" column is the most important one since it's especially designed to counteract avoidance. If we do nothing else, we can still mark off this column. This may not be an impressive accomplishment. But by focusing on our tasks, we are challenging our avoidance. If we do this long enough, eventually we will get around to tackling what must be done.

The self-management chart is very versatile. It can be as long as we want and include any activity. If the tasks are realistic and we check the chart every day, it will help us keep our mind on the project.

Reward

Psychologists speaking of reward or reinforcement often bring to mind images of children receiving M&Ms for putting round pegs into round holes or white rats receiving food pellets for pressing knobs in their cages. While candy and pellets may be needed to motivate children and rats, most adults wouldn't consider the idea of systematically rewarding themselves.

Nevertheless, a great deal of research documents the importance of reinforcement in controlling behavior. For example, one researcher found that women who were taught to reward themselves for assertive group participation were more active in group discussion than women who received assertiveness training without the reinforcement component.[3]

Moreover, from the perspective of women's issues, there is an additional reason for using reward to help us follow through. Building in reinforcement is an excellent method of giving ourselves *recognition*. It's a means of acknowledging that we have completed steps and achieved goals. It's a way of focusing on our accomplishments and giving ourselves credit for them. This way we strike a blow at the feminine discounting habit.

We should select rewards that are realistic and motivating but not indispensable. If the rewards are too valuable, we risk the temptation of cheating and defeating our good intentions. And we should give ourselves reinforcement for desirable behavior and *withhold* reinforcement in its absence.

The variety of rewards is endless. Here are just some examples.

- listening to music
- watching television
- going shopping
- gardening
- having lunch with a friend
- having a facial
- eating favorite foods
- going to the movies
- partying
- traveling
- buying jewelry
- reading
- getting a massage
- dancing
- attending a concert
- playing sports
- doing nothing

Reinforcement is most effective when it follows closely on the heels of desired behavior. For example, if you want to reward yourself for speaking up at staff meetings, it's better to reinforce yourself immediately after the assertion than a day or two later. Immediacy is particularly important when doing something anxiety provoking or trying to change well-established habits.

This poses an obvious problem. Most of the time, it isn't practical to treat ourselves immediately. We can't stop the action and give ourselves a facial or buy a pair of earrings.

Fortunately, there are ways around this problem. First, we can reward ourselves with praise. We can acknowledge our accomplishments in our self-talk. We can say such things as "I *did* it." Or "Nice work!" Or "I am glad I stayed with it, it's really paid off."

Such congratulatory self-talk is powerful and always available. And importantly, it's incompatible with discounting. It kills two birds with one stone: It reinforces desirable behavior and helps to undermine the feminine discounting habit.

A second way around the immediacy problem is to use symbols to bridge the gap between current behavior and future reward. Remember how we were awarded gold stars in school? The kid with the most got a reward at the end of the week. Now, instead of giving ourselves gold stars, we give ourselves points that we can "redeem" for rewards at our convenience. For example, if you are trying to increase your assertiveness, you can give yourself a point for each assertive action. Having decided beforehand the value of each point, you can spend it on a small reward, such as a manicure, or you can save up points for big treats: ten points for a new pocketbook or fifty points for a trip to Bermuda. Or you can do both: Give yourself daily rewards and then big treats when you pass milestones in your project.

Another thing to keep in mind when planning reinforcement is the idea of "early and often." Initially, we should reward ourselves for taking even the smallest steps. For example, if our first task is simply to write our name on an application form, we should give ourselves both praise and points for doing so. This will make the next steps seem more appealing. As we go along, we can raise our standard for reinforcement; but remember, it's better to err on the side of too much reward than too little.

Even when we don't establish a formal reward system, we should actively praise ourselves for accomplishments. This builds up self-esteem and reduces excessive dependency on the approval of others.

Accountability

We have already seen the value of building in accountability by checking in regularly with a "collaborator." It's best to establish this at the beginning of the project and to make the contact an integral part of it.

Generally speaking, a weekly check-in is a good policy. However, when the tasks are particularly difficult or stressful, it can be useful to check in more often. Knowing that someone is expecting frequent progress reports can spur us on to action—if for no other reason than to avoid embarrassment.

Accountability can be aided by the use of written agreements signed by you and your collaborator. If you don't plan to have a collaborator, you can make a contract with yourself. The agreement should spell out: (1) your goal, (2) what you intend to do, (3) when or how often you intend to do it, and, optionally, (4) how you plan to reward yourself for holding to your commitment, and (5) consequences for noncompliance. Here is a sample:

Research suggests that people who make written agreements are more effective in managing their target behavior than those who don't. One study found that students who wrote out contracts in which they promised themselves to study for and take the many quizzes in the course took more tests and were better prepared than those students who hadn't made written agreements.[4]

Contract

Goal: To get job as a technical writer in growing company.

Agreement:

I, Mary Jane Smith, agree to engage in activity essential to finding a new position. This includes such things as reworking my résumé, making phone calls, writing letters, reading classifieds, networking, interviewing, and doing research on the job market.

I will begin on March 7, 1990, and stop when I have accepted a job offer.

I intend to do one job-search-related task each day, from Monday to Friday.

For each task I complete, I will give myself one point. If I do more than one a day, I will give myself double points. I will redeem my points for daily rewards and when I have acquired fifty points I will treat myself to a Cuisinart.

For each task I shirk, I will donate one dollar to a local charity.

I will check in with my collaborator every Friday to report my week's progress.

Signed: *Mary Jane Smith*
_____

Ruth Brown
_____
Collaborator

Date: March 5, 1990

Keeping Energy Up

Taking action can be taxing. Success in following through is often related to how well we manage our energy and deal with stress. Unfortunately, one of the most common complaints among contemporary women is that of fatigue. Many of us feel tired too often. This is no small matter. Cars don't run on EMPTY and neither do we.

Three excellent methods for keeping energy up and handling tension are exercise, deep muscle relaxation, and good nutrition.

Exercise. Swimming, jogging, and dancing are some perennial favorite forms of exercise that relieve tension. Exercise not only helps us unwind, it produces biochemical changes that can relieve and prevent anxiety and depression.

In addition to its beneficial physical effects, exercise can increase our sense of well-being by contributing to our perception of control. Awareness of our growing ability to master our bodies often leads to greater self-confidence and a better self-image. A research study found that athletic college coeds had higher scores on a self-image test than did other women.[5]

By increasing our energy and confidence, exercise can improve our efficiency and effectiveness. Research suggests that it may improve mental functioning and even stimulate the imagination.[6] This connection is important to people concerned about productivity. Corporations are increasingly providing employees with gyms and physical fitness programs. Executives consider these to be investments that will pay off in improved morale and increased productivity. So should we.

Relaxation. Has your stomach ever been tied in knots? Your neck? Back? If you find yourself feeling this way too often, deep muscle relaxation is for you. This technique has become popular in recent years and has been incorporated into many stress-management programs.

Basically, the idea is to tense and then relax sets of muscles. By doing this the muscles relax more deeply than they did before they were tensed. This also teaches us to be more aware of how muscle tension feels, making it easier to spot in daily life.

With practice it's possible to learn to control our muscles so that we can produce relaxation on command, at the first signs of tension, simply by relaxing one set of muscles and telling ourselves "Relax" or "Calm."

In order to learn this, you need to practice once a day on a comfortable chair or bed in a private, quiet place that's free of distractions or interruptions.

Take deep breaths and systematically hold the tension for five to seven seconds and then relax for twenty to thirty seconds. It will take about thirty minutes to do the following:

1. Hands
   a. Clench dominant hand
      Relax it
   b. Clench other hand
      Relax it
2. Arms
   a. Tighten dominant upper arm and shoulder
      Relax them
   b. Tighten other upper arm and shoulder
      Relax them
3. Face
   a. Raise eyebrows as high as possible
      Lower them
   b. With eyes closed, roll eyes up; then down
      Relax them

    c. With eyes closed, clench eyelids
       Unclench them
    d. Wrinkle nose
       Unwrinkle it
    e. With mouth closed, stretch lips to ears
       Relax mouth
    f. Press tongue against teeth
       Release it
    g. Clench jaw
       Relax it

4. Neck
    a. Put head on left shoulder
       Bring it back to upright position
    b. Put head on right shoulder
       Bring upright
    c. Roll head back
       Bring upright
    d. Touch chin to chest
       Bring upright

5. Chest
    a. Pull shoulders back all the way
       Let arms hang loose
    b. Pull shoulders forward all the way
       Let arms hang loose

6. Stomach
    a. Tighten
       Relax it

7. Buttocks
    a. Tighten
       Relax them

8. Legs
    a. Tighten right thigh
       Relax it
    b. Tighten left thigh
       Relax it

  c. Tighten right calf
     Relax it
  d. Tighten left calf
     Relax it
  e. Point toes away from you
     Relax them
  f. Point toes toward you
     Relax them

Once you know the exercises well, you can practice tensing and relaxing sets of muscles in other situations. Choose a variety of different settings.

There are many ways of using relaxation to deal with tension. It can be used to unwind after work or before going to bed. It can also function as an all-purpose coping device before and during stressful activities such as interviews, meetings, and exams.

Deep muscle relaxation is by no means the only way to calm down. The advantage of deep muscle relaxation, however, is its versatility and handiness in a variety of stressful situations.

Nutrition. Joan, a thirty-year-old manager, came to counseling complaining of loss of self-confidence at work. Her distress was connected to an unpleasant situation: A small group of employees were dissatisfied and actively bad-mouthing her performance.

What puzzled Joan was that she was so upset. She had strong support from her superiors and her fourteen other subordinates. Her rational mind told her to take the whole thing in stride. Yet she felt unable to do so. Not usually a worrier, Joan spent leisure time preoccupied with the tempest in the teapot.

In addition, Joan complained of a great deal of fatigue. Sometimes when she came home from work she was too tired to make dinner and didn't eat at all. By 8:00 P.M. she was ready to turn in.

When Joan discussed her diet, her fatigue and low stress tolerance began to make sense. She described what she had consumed that day: two cups of coffee, three cans of diet soda, and several handfuls of peanuts. For dinner, she was looking forward to Stouffer's Lean Cuisine. Even worse, this was a typical day; she had been eating this way for years.

Joan is like many women who don't take adequate care of their nutrition. Very often, in a time crunch, good nutrition is one of the first things to go. Even many women who do pay attention to their diets are concerned primarily with losing weight rather than with healthy food. The effects of this will be seen sooner or later in fatigue, irritability, inefficiency, and illness.

The obvious solution is to pay attention to what we eat. When we are trying to follow through on major projects, we ought to think of ourselves as athletes in training. We should eat foods that give us the most energy and avoid those that deplete our resources, such as refined sugars, caffeinated drinks, and liquor. Women who have problems with anxiety, depression, or hypoglycemia need to be particularly careful about diet.

It has been said that an army travels on its stomach. Well, we do too.

EVALUATING

If we wanted to know the distance from New York to San Francisco, it wouldn't do us much good to stretch our yardstick across the Atlantic. Absurd as this may sound, that's exactly how some people evaluate their progress.

They measure the distance between their current position and their ultimate, sometimes ideal, goal. That, however, tells them only what they have left to accomplish, not *what they have already achieved*. Other people prefer not to think about their starting point because it makes them feel bad about themselves. Whatever the reason, this is inaccurate and it undermines self-esteem because it discounts progress.

The only way to evaluate our progress is to compare our current position with our starting point: How far have we gotten from square one?

A trap many of us fall into is underestimating our progress because we adapt rapidly to higher levels of performance. We quickly forget humble beginnings and take our current level of functioning for granted, like marathon runners who don't recall how they huffed and puffed through their first miles. Gradually, almost without our awareness, our expectations shift upward with our competence. We set our sights higher, to newer and bigger challenges, without noticing how much we have grown.

In order to evaluate accurately, we should review our diaries and charts, and ask ourselves some questions.

- Where was my starting point?
- Where am I now?
- Did I achieve my goals?
- Have I examined all possible signs of improvement?
- Have I learned anything?

If we are satisfied with our progress, we can move along and evaluate weekly, or as the need arises.

If we ran into trouble, we need to troubleshoot.

- What interfered with achieving my goals?
- When and where did I encounter problems?
- How might they be prevented in the future?
- Did I try my hardest?
- Were my goals realistic?

After assessing our difficulties, we can modify our plan to work around obstacles.

QUICK REVIEW

To sum up the last two chapters, when we are stuck, the way to get moving and to tackle tasks is to:

1. Describe our goal positively and precisely.
2. Focus on the tasks by making a detailed list of all that needs to be done to achieve the goal.
3. Organize the tasks into small steps and create mini-goals.
4. Arrange those steps in a sequence that begins with the most comfortable step and ends with the least comfortable one.
5. Schedule the tasks.
6. Use warm-ups.
7. Keep focused on tasks with the self-management chart.
8. Build in rewards.
9. Become accountable to someone else.
10. Keep energy up and tension down with exercise, relaxation, and good nutrition.
11. Evaluate accurately.

All this takes time and effort. But we have a plan and we can get there from here.

CHAPTER 9

Managing Thoughts

In the normal course of events we take our thinking for granted. But when tackling problematic projects, the brain sometimes generates unproductive thoughts that masquerade as sensible ideas. Since these deceptive thoughts impede our moving forward, frequently bringing progress to a halt altogether, we have to learn to control them.

Some people believe there is something unnatural about trying to manage one's own thoughts. They see the mind in a romanticized way, as a mystical force that shouldn't be tampered with. They view attempts at imposing structure on one's thinking as artificial and restrictive.

In fact, the opposite is true. Eliminating self-defeating thoughts is a liberating experience.

For those who wish to gain greater self-control, it's practical to consider thinking as being simply another form of behavior. This way we can apply behavioral self-management principles, which have been used successfully to change other types of behavior, to our thought processes.

SELF-TALK

Self-talk is a term used to describe people's ongoing internal dialogues. It refers to the running commentary we make to ourselves as we go through the day; the minute-to-minute instructions we give ourselves, and the minute-to-minute evaluations we make of our behavior and environment. For example, imagine playing a game of tennis. You might say to yourself:

- "Give it all you've got," as you serve the ball.
- "Hit it to her backhand; she's weak there."
- "Good shot," as you follow through.
- "Damn, there's a hole in my racquet," as you miss the return.

Let's take another example. You are driving in your car and the traffic light turns yellow. You might say to yourself:

- "I've got to brake and slow down."
- Or "I'd better step on the accelerator so I can make it before the light turns red."

Self-talk isn't scintillating conversation. It is made up of mundane, commonplace, habitual thoughts. And because these are so routine, a good deal of the time we are totally oblivious to them. Nonetheless, self-talk isn't an unconscious process; retrieving it doesn't require years in psychoanalysis. Self-talk is thought content we have learned to ignore because it allows us to devote attention to our activities. But, as we shall see later, we can become aware of our self-talk when we choose to.

Helpless Self-Talk

Without a doubt, the greatest psychological barrier to effective action is helpless self-talk. The difference between successful women and those of comparable abilities and circumstances who get stuck is the amount of learned helplessness they carry with them. Those of us who procrastinate a great deal, who can't get started at all, or who have trouble following through have far too many helpless thoughts circulating in our heads.

Claudette, for example, wanted to attend a two-week summer art program. Although the program was filled up, she was encouraged to submit an application and be placed on a waiting list. But she couldn't get herself to do it. Her self-talk went like this: "It's hopeless. I will never get into the program. There is such a long waiting list. Even if there were an opening, I wouldn't get in. My work isn't good enough. It isn't professional enough."

Whenever motivated women fail to initiate action or to persist, the inaction is always preceded by helpless self-talk. This follows as surely as night follows day. Hundreds of women of different ages, backgrounds, life-styles, goals, and projects have shared their thoughts with me. Despite their diversity, they have essentially the same self-talk: "I can't do it. It won't work."

Learned helplessness operates in our daily lives by infecting our self-talk with the automatic thought that there is little we can do to achieve our goals. The operative word is "automatic." Whereas realistic self-talk reflects an accurate judgment of current reality, automatic thoughts represent a short circuit in the evaluation process. The brain, instead of actively processing new information and generating reasonable appraisals, goes on automatic pilot and replays the old tapes of learned helplessness that say "I can't do it." We, however, imagine we are receiving an accurate assessment of our situation. We assume our self-talk is providing a reasonable guideline for action, and we act on it. Or, to be more precise, we don't act; we don't get started or we quit prematurely. Were we processing information correctly, we might still come up with "It can't be done." But this would be a warranted conclusion, arrived at after serious attempts at problem solving.

The misfortune of learned helplessness is that it short-circuits the problem-solving process by producing an automatic response. This knee-jerk reaction of "It won't work" prevents an accurate evaluation, and we miss the opportunity to discover what we really could accomplish.

While helpless self-talk is the centerpiece in the display of unproductive thinking, there are several related habits that also obstruct action: worry, avoidance, and excessive self-criticism.

Worry

If learned helplessness were a family, helpless self-talk and worry would be fraternal twins. Both are types of unproductive thinking. But while helpless thoughts concern a current situation, worry is helplessness projected into the future. It is self-talk about an event that hasn't happened yet, but might occur at some point down the road. It takes the following form:

- "What if ——— [fill in the blank] happens?"
- "What will I do?"

The first question assumes the unwelcome event is highly probable. Often this is a questionable assumption. However, even when there is a good chance of the dreaded event happening, the second question isn't the beginning of a creative problem-solving process. It is a rephrasing of classic helpless thinking: "I can't handle it."

Ruth, a woman who designs and makes silver jewelry,

worries a great deal about money. Earning just enough to get by, she describes herself as "not initiating business" and "just plodding along." She is a reserved woman who doesn't like to go out and sell, but neither does she like her hand-to-mouth existence. Using the strategies in Chapter 8, Ruth applied for admission to several prestigious shows in the crafts circuit.

Despite stiff competition, she got accepted to the two best shows. At first she was ecstatic. Then panic set in. Her head became flooded with worries: "I want to make it. Can I? Can I have a *real* business? The shows are so expensive. It's going to cost my last red cent. What if the car breaks down again? I couldn't afford to repair it. What if I can't make money at the shows? I will really be in a hole. I can't ask my sister again. She needs her money. I am forty-six years old and have no financial security. What if the show doesn't make money? What will I do?"

When worrying, we might imagine we are problem solving because we are anticipating future difficulties: Forewarned is forearmed. There is, however, a world of difference between problem solving and worrying.

In the mastery-oriented mindset we believe we have a good chance of handling difficulties, self-talk is geared to foster creativity and generate new ideas, and the mind searches for solutions. Energy is directed toward productive action. And although we may not feel deliriously happy when tackling problems, we do have a real sense of feeling alive.

By way of marked contrast, in the worried mindset we don't believe we can handle the anticipated situation. Our thoughts consist of repetitious rehearsals of the problem, rather than of creative ideas for the solution. Tension is high, energy is unfocused, and the net result is a sense of feeling drained.

Some of us, perhaps believing that we are problem solving, substitute worry for work. Instead of making jewelry, writing an annual report, or studying constitutional law, we think about consequences. What happens if the jewelry doesn't sell, the boss doesn't like the report, or we flunk the constitutional law exam? However, *thinking about possible failure is not thinking about work*. While this may appear to be an obvious point, too many women don't get it. We imagine that if we are thinking about any aspect of work life, we are being productive. This is not the case. If we are worrying about failing, we are not thinking about jewelry, reports, or law. Worrying is, with respect to the tasks at hand, the functional equivalent of "gone fishin'."

Avoidance

Fear of failure, as discussed earlier, causes some of us to develop a motive to avoid work. It's as if an inner force pulls us away from our tasks, like an undertow pulling a swimmer away from the shore. When we don't fight this force, our projects drown.

Avoidance self-talk often *conceals* as well as facilitates avoidance behavior. When not alert, we can fool ourselves. This was the case with Shelley, a graduate student, who said to herself, "I'm too tired to make dinner and then go all the way back to the library. I'll study at home tonight. It's such an awful night out anyway." By ignoring the fact that she works effectively only in the library, not at home, Shelley conned herself into believing she was going to study, while she was actually preparing to play hooky.

The most blatant type of avoidance self-talk is the rationalization. We deliberately choose to *not* do something we had previously intended to do—write a report, make a phone call, chastise a subordinate—and then we give ourselves seemingly plausible excuses for our change of heart. Some common ones are: "I'm too tired," "There's not enough time," "It's not so important anyway," "It can wait," and "I've wasted most of the evening, it's too late to start now."

Instead of actively making excuses, we can just "happen to" get involved with something else. Meg, for example, while struggling with her income taxes, said to herself, "I can't figure this out. What a bore. I wonder if there is any apple pie left." Abandoning her 1040EZ, she went off to the kitchen and avoided, for the moment, the chore of doing taxes. Eating, watching television, and reading are time-honored methods for avoidance at home; but even at the office we have our ways. When all else fails, "I need a cup of coffee" or "I have to go to the john" is the self-talk that organizes the escape.

Finally, avoidance self-talk can take the form of the chronic "existential crisis," in which we distract ourselves with conversations that go something like this: "Why am I struggling so hard? Am I running a fool's errand? Where is my life going? Have I made the right choice? Would I be happier doing something else?" This type of dialogue can go on indefinitely and be called to mind whenever the going gets rough. Unlike an authentic crisis of commitment, which occurs infrequently and genuinely evaluates the undertaking, the chronic existential crisis is merely the replay of an old tape that functions as avoidance.

Excessive Self-Criticism

It's one thing to analyze and to constructively criticize our actions. It's quite another to automatically beat ourselves up every time we miss perfection by a hair. Needlessly harsh self-talk amounts to self-abuse. Here are some examples:

- "My God, I don't have any control over my mouth; I ought to be gagged before going out in public."
- "I really did it this time. Here is the department's most important project and I got careless. I

should have caught that error. Instead, I just proved, once more, how incompetent I am."
- "Why aren't I livening up this conversation? It's my fault everyone's bored. I have as much social savvy as a snail."

Imagine how it would feel if another person called you incompetent. It isn't any more fun when you do it to yourself. If you have any questions about whether or not your self-talk is abusive, ask yourself, "Would I say this to another person I care about? And, if I did, would she be offended?"

Self-critical self-talk can create stress. This was demonstrated beautifully in a simple experiment. Researchers asked one group of students to read critical statements to themselves and a second group to read neutral ones.[1] While they were reading, physiological measures indicating stress were taken. Only the students reading the critical statements were emotionally aroused. Despite the fact they were merely reading material supplied by a stranger in an impersonal situation, they reacted with stress.

Self-abusive and helpless self-talk often go hand in hand. When we feel distressed by feelings of powerlessness and vulnerability, helpless thoughts may become cues for beating on ourselves. This was the case with one woman who was laid off. While contemplating her job hunt she said to herself, "It's my fault I was laid off. Something is wrong with me. I never do anything right. I don't have what it takes to do technical work. I am always messing up. I am not productive. I am no good for anything."

Unfortunately, destructive self-criticism makes helpless thinking more difficult to cope with. If we respond to helpless thoughts with self-abuse, there is a rapid progression from a feeling of helplessness to a feeling of despair. Having beaten ourselves up, we are left with pulverized self-confidence, little energy, and zero enthusiasm. Moreover, fear of failure increases when we anticipate punishment from ourselves every time we miscalculate. Taking action in this frame of mind is difficult, to say the least.

CHANGING SELF-TALK

"In a real sense through our own self-talk we are either in the construction business or the wrecking business."[2]

We have seen how the wrecking crews of the mind operate: They make unreasonable demands and are excessively harsh in their criticism, play inaccurate old tapes, organize sit-down strikes, and generally obstruct productive action. Now that we understand how profoundly destructive this wrecking business is, we can stop tearing ourselves down and start building ourselves up.

Behavioral strategies are the key to creating constructive thinking habits. They assist us in altering thought patterns by providing specific activities that give logic and order to the process of changing our thoughts. In doing so they transform the somewhat vague business of thinking into a more controllable operation.

Our game plan is to learn to substitute productive thoughts for self-defeating ones, to make the switch *before* the negative self-talk takes us down the wrong road. The challenges are to become aware of the unwanted thoughts, recognize them quickly, and then intervene effectively. This is done in two phases: tuning in and talking back.

Tuning In

Upon learning the concept of self-talk, most of us recognize it immediately as something we do all the time. We can tune in and "hear" ourselves talk quite easily. However, since ignoring self-talk allows us to concentrate on our activities, the task becomes one of *selective listening*.

The way we conceptualize our problem will dictate how

we tune in to our thoughts. Negative self-talk can be a specific reaction to a particular set of circumstances or a characteristic response to a broad variety of life's stresses.

If we believe we have a problem with a particular set of circumstances, we monitor our self-talk only in that problematic situation. For example, a lawyer was puzzled by her recent difficulty getting up in the morning. Observing her thoughts on awakening, she found that she was visualizing a courtroom, experiencing a tightening in her stomach, and saying to herself, "What am I doing here?" Tuning in to her thoughts made it clear she was having trouble getting up because she didn't want to face a disagreeable trial.

Amanda used this troubleshooting technique in her job hunt. Although she was tired of slaving in "the coal mines," as she referred to the brokerage house where she worked, she was wiling away her evenings instead of writing cover letters for her résumé. Tuning in to her thoughts showed why. Amanda kept a diary of her self-talk during the period between dinner and bedtime, which solved the puzzle of the unwritten letters. Here are some samples from her diary: "I don't know what to say in this letter," "Is it really going to work?" "I don't know if I can do the job if I get it," and "If I start this now, I'll miss *Cheers*."

Alternatively, we might be concerned about our responses to life in general. Do we frequently respond to the vicissitudes of life with helplessness or self-abuse? In this case, instead of observing specific situations, we instruct ourselves to be alert to self-defeating thoughts that crop up during the course of our everyday lives. When we hear a self-defeating thought, it should be recorded in our diary, and whenever possible, the situation that prompted the negative thought and the feelings or behavior that followed it should be described. Here are examples from the diaries of women who were tuning in to helpless thinking during the course of a typical week:

- A financial analyst submitted an article to a journal and received a response indicating that the editor either didn't understand or didn't like what she had written. She thought, "All my efforts are doomed to failure," and became depressed.
- A product manager was informed that she would be traveling around the country speaking to executives and thought "Who am I to talk to all these executives?" and started panicking.
- A student taking a course in acting had a small part in the class play. As she waited offstage, she thought to herself, "What if I forget my lines?" and began comparing herself unfavorably to other class members.

Scanning our self-talk can pinpoint problems and thus pave the way to solutions. Christina and her daughter Terry, age fourteen, learned this when they made a pact to monitor their self-deprecating language. Terry's diary revealed that most of her put-downs occurred during math class and homework. This highlighted a subtle problem. Although Terry achieved good grades in math, it didn't come as easily as did other subjects. At times math was difficult and this made her feel inadequate and prompted excessively self-critical thoughts. Her negative self-talk was really a red flag signaling trouble. Once she discovered this, she realized she wasn't inadequate, she simply needed to work harder than usual. As a result, she paid more attention to math and the self-deprecation stopped.

Unlike Terry, some women are so chronically self-critical that anything can trigger off a barrage of abuse. The wind changes direction and they blame it on themselves. Under these circumstances, the target of concern is not the content and context of the self-talk but its *frequency*. In this case, an alternative technique for self-monitoring is more efficient. Instead of writing details in a daily diary, we simply *count* the number of negative thoughts that flicker through our minds in the course of the day. This can be done easily with the aid of a mechanical device such as a golf scorer (which can be worn like a watch and be purchased at sporting goods stores) or a knitting stitch counter. The device keeps track of the total and all we need do is record it on a daily and weekly basis.

Through self-monitoring, we become alert to self-defeating thoughts and learn to recognize them quickly. In the process, some thoughts will disappear spontaneously due to the phenomenon of reactivity (recall Chapter 7). The remaining thoughts will need more work.

Talking Back

Listening to ourselves creates the opportunity to change our conversational gambits: to eliminate the negative and emphasize the productive.

Notice I didn't say emphasize the *positive*. Let me explain. Contrary to what many people believe, we don't have to think positively. It isn't always possible. Sometimes we are too discouraged, frustrated, anxious, or uninspired to be optimistic. Under these circumstances it's too big a step to move from negative to positive thoughts. Fortunately, it's enough to shift from negative to neutral. We don't have to say "Yes, I can," we just have to say "Well, maybe." As long as we don't automatically say "No can do," we are all right.

Thought Stopping.   Dr. Joseph Wolpe developed what has become the classic behavioral technique for eliminating unwanted thoughts. Thought stopping is the major skill that must be acquired to effectively manage self-talk. Once it is learned it can be combined with other techniques to help us curb worry, silence excessive self-criticism, and counter helplessness and avoidance.

Thought stopping is a procedure that consists of interrupting unwanted thoughts and then systematically re-placing them with other thoughts. It requires both planning and practice. Let's look at an example to see how it is done. Recall Ruth, the jewelry designer who worried about her success at the upcoming craft show. She learned thought stopping to prevent herself from dwelling on the possibility of failure. Here is what she did:

1. Ruth began by bringing on the unwanted thought: "What if the show doesn't make money? What will I do? I am forty-six years old and I have no financial security." Bringing on the unwanted thought is a way of taking charge, of saying "I can command my thoughts. I can think them when I want to and dismiss them when I don't."
2. Her next step was to interrupt the unwanted thought. She did this by *shouting* "STOP!" The action of shouting out loud, strange thought it may be, is effective because it is impossible to ignore.
3. Immediately after shouting "STOP!" she *substituted* a pleasant scene: walking around a secluded lake in Maine.

Ruth practiced these three steps for ten minutes each day in a private place where she felt comfortable shouting. She practiced until she became skilled at substituting thoughts on command. Then, instead of shouting out loud, she said "STOP!" to herself. To insure she wouldn't ignore the command to stop, she gently snapped a rubber band on her wrist. These changes made it possible to do thought stopping in public places.

There are several ways to create the substitution. The first is to make a list, in advance, of ten scenes. They can be real experiences or fantasies. Here are some examples:

1. The beach at sunset.
2. Horseback riding.
3. Working in the garden.

4. A scene from the movie *Out of Africa*.
5. Baking bread.
6. The canals of Venice.
7. The *Nutcracker* at Christmas.
8. My dream house, an old Victorian, full of nooks and crannies.
9. My daughter finger painting.
10. Sitting around a fireplace with friends, and eating, drinking, and laughing.

It doesn't matter what we substitute; it can be the Lord's Prayer or an erotic fantasy. The crucial point is that it not be negative or distressing. For example, one woman complained that thought stopping wasn't working for her. When she described her substitutions, the reason became clear. In an attempt to eliminate self-defeating thoughts about her imagined inability to survive in the corporate jungle, she substituted a romantic scene: dancing in the moonlight with a handsome man. This scene, however, reminded her that she lacked a romantic relationship and made her feel miserable.

She had essentially replaced a headache with an upset stomach. If the content of the substitution leads to painful thoughts, drop it and concentrate on something neutral or positive.

Another method of switching thoughts is to count backward from ten. Do this until the unwanted thoughts are gone. Some people like to combine both methods: They begin by counting backward and then substitute a scene. Use whatever method you find the easiest. If you aren't sure, experiment until you find what works for you.

Do thought stopping early and often. Do it every time unwanted thoughts creep into your awareness. Start as soon as the self-defeating thoughts begin. The sooner you catch yourself, the less likely you are to bring yourself down.

Curbing Worry

Why make ourselves miserable by worrying repeatedly in the course of the day? We can do it more efficiently by consolidating it all into one block of "worry time."

Schedule a block of twenty minutes at a regular time each day and use that time to review all your worries. Sort out the solvable problems from the unsolvable ones, then try to arrive at some solutions. During the course of the day, save up your worries for that special time. If you fear forgetting important points, write them down. Use thought stopping when necessary to keep from worrying at un-scheduled times.

Do your worrying in the same place. Find a particular chair (don't use your favorite chair lest it become associated with worries) in a particular location, and use this spot exclusively. The point is to restrict worrying so it doesn't contaminate other areas of your life.

In the past, Marilyn had always played it safe. The problem was that after several years of an assortment of "safe" jobs, she was bored and frustrated. They offered low pay and little challenge. Torn by a desire to succeed and by an equally strong fear of failure, she felt stuck. To make matters worse, her husband was tired of hearing about her career conflicts and was pressuring her to make a good decision.

Then came the offer. It was a challenging job in an employment agency where, if successful, she could make a great deal of money. It was both exciting and scary. High risks, high profits.

Marilyn took the plunge. But the minute she accepted the job, her anxiety skyrocketed. She became obsessed with work. Evenings and weekends were dominated with wor-ries about meeting her quota of placements. She began to feel as if she had no life outside of the office.

She reported that her self-talk went like this: "I haven't

placed anyone yet. It's already been two weeks. What happens if I don't place someone soon? I have three to six months to prove myself. What if I don't make it? Have I made a mistake? I should have stuck to word processing. It's always dangerous to try something new. Whatever made me think I could do it? I must have been crazy to let that smooth operator talk me into this. Now I am in a mess. What if I fail?"

In order to give herself and her job a fair chance, Marilyn decided to try the "worry time" strategy. She monitored her worried thoughts during the day and spent twenty minutes every night on a dining room chair facing the wall, reviewing her anxieties about failing at her job.

Along with these activities she practiced thought stopping, and after several weeks she had mastered thought stopping so effectively she was able to shut off her unwanted thoughts immediately. To her delight, she had much less to think about at worry time. Freeing herself from unproductive thoughts allowed Marilyn to be more effective in her work and to enjoy her leisure.

Silencing Self-Criticism

Although constructive self-criticism isn't fun, it has a self-correcting function. Mistakes and failures can become valuable sources of knowledge when we honestly appraise and learn from them. When this process has gone awry and we beat ourselves instead of being constructive, the self-abuse should be stopped. We do this by becoming aware of it and then terminating it with thought stopping.

If the abuse has become habitual, further steps need be taken. This was the case with twenty-seven-year-old Lisa, who came into counseling feeling anxious and depressed. Nothing in her life seemed to be going right.

She had followed her fiancé to Boston only to find that their relationship was in trouble. Further, due to an economic recession, she had difficulty finding work and felt compelled to take a job that she described as "banal." As the bright, talented daughter of a wealthy lawyer, she had expected to find interesting work. Now she felt stuck in a dead-end clerical job that wore down her self-esteem.

Lisa made matters worse by being excessively self-critical. She needed to attend to her internal dialogues and produce a more upbeat script. Eliminating abusive self-talk became her target goal.

Lisa began by keeping a daily diary of all her self-critical thoughts and the circumstances in which they occurred in order to determine if the self-abuse was a reaction to specific types of situations. In the first week, she recorded forty-three self-critical remarks.

In reviewing her diary after a week, Lisa realized her self-abuse was a knee-jerk response to any and all frustration and that the content of the self-talk was fairly predictable. Since the context and the content of the self-talk weren't noteworthy, she decided to use a golf scorer, instead of a diary, to keep track of what she called her "nasties."

In the next several weeks, in addition to counting nasties, Lisa practiced thought stopping. After acquiring this skill, Lisa decided to reduce her self-abusive thoughts by three a week. She set her first minigoal at forty and then continued reducing her nasties by three per week. As she got closer to her target goal, the task became increasingly difficult. Consequently she reduced the rate at which she cut down her self-abusive thoughts from three per week to two, and later from two to one.

Strange as it may seem, as the self-abusive thoughts decreased, Lisa felt an emptiness: Something was missing. To fill this void, she monitored her positive thinking. Every time she had a pleasant thought or experience, she made an entry in her diary. No good thought was too trivial: "A delicious tuna sandwich," "Great, I missed the rush hour traffic," "What a lovely sunset."

Like many negative thinkers, Lisa loved the "good news" diary and found that her positive thoughts multiplied. As they increased, Lisa switched to simply keeping a tally of upbeat thoughts.

It took Lisa six months to eliminate excessively critical self-talk. However, it returned periodically when Lisa was under severe stress. Then her self-abusive thoughts would start up like a case of hives. Nevertheless, she was able to use this pattern to her advantage. She learned to treat the self-abuse as a cue to problem solve: to step back, look at her stress, and to do something about it. The excessively self-critical self-talk changed from a knee-jerk reflex to a useful warning signal.

Countering Helplessness and Avoidance

Sometimes it isn't enough to silence negative self-talk. We want thinking that will work for us and help us work. We need productive thoughts: accurate, reasonable, and facilitating action.

Good self-talk can be generated through the process of *countering*. Instead of listening uncritically and acting blindly, we challenge our unproductive self-talk with questions and assertions. For example, Angela, who just started a job as a production manager at a public relations firm, had plenty of experience handling a $10,000 budget, but responded helplessly to the task of handling a $100,000 one. But, instead of losing herself in helpless thoughts, she tuned in to her self-talk and said "STOP!" Then she countered with: "Well, *why* can't I?" "How do I know I can't do it? I haven't tried yet." "Have I ever done anything like this before?" Questions such as these help us to gain a more realistic assessment of our situation.

When we suspect avoidance tactics we should cross-examine ourselves. As we observe ourselves picking up a magazine, turning on the television, or trotting off to the coffee machine, we should say "STOP! Do I really need a break now? Will it help my work or make me further behind?" When Kate was working on a presentation at 8:00 P.M., she marked her self-talk: "I feel so sleepy. I think I will work on this tomorrow." She immediately became suspicious of her motives because her normal bedtime was eleven o'clock. She said "STOP!" and countered with: "Am I really tired, or would I revive in a minute if my love dropped by with two concert tickets?" "Yes, this can wait until tomorrow, but won't I have even more work then?"

These are genuine questions that, depending on the situation, could go either way. There are occasions when we feel tired, hungry, or just need time out. Letting ourselves off the hook is legitimate under these circumstances. But usually we know when we are being straight and when we are avoiding work. A student with poor study habits said of herself, "Talking to myself works with dieting. I think about the long-term gains of not eating and often I can get myself to stop. But I have never tried that with studying. I just decide not to do it and that's that. I never challenge my decision." Once she started countering her avoidance, her study habits and her grades improved.

A more definitive counter is an assertion that our self-talk is inaccurate, illogical, unreasonable, or in some other way faulty. When we are sure we are selling ourselves a bill of goods, we can reject it. We talk back to helpless thoughts by asserting "I have done similar kinds of things before, and I can probably do this now." Or "I always make a fuss and then I do fine." Or "It doesn't follow that because I messed up once, I am doomed to perpetual failure." Talking back to avoidance is simple: "This is avoidance, it's impeding my progress, so let's get to work." An all-purpose counter that can be used on almost any occasion is "This thought is pointless. It doesn't help me accomplish my goals."

Learning to challenge the lines we hand ourselves will help us cope with specific situations. But even more important, countering unproductive thoughts will change the general direction of our thinking and foster the development of mastery-oriented behavior.

CHAPTER 10

Changing Patterns

We have now learned how to modify self-talk. But what about other behavior patterns that need to be altered?

When we tackle tasks the aim is to produce a product or a situation: a line of jewelry, a magazine article, or a new job. However, the same logic used in tackling tasks can be applied to changing routine behavior patterns such as self-assertion, work habits, and stress management. We break down the target behavior into minigoals and systematically work toward accomplishing them. We begin with the easiest goal and finish with the most difficult. Additional strategies and techniques can be used wherever needed.

To formulate goals, we ask ourselves two basic questions: (1) "What do I want to do more of?" and (2) "What do I want to do less of?" Once these questions have been answered we can develop a plan.

What Jenny wanted was to be more assertive at work. An extremely anxious twenty-three-year-old research assistant, the only woman in the geology department of a prestigious university, Jenny felt hopelessly tongue-tied at staff meetings. She didn't need to monitor her group participation to know she opened her mouth only when asked a direct question. Embarrassed by her awkwardness, she felt eager to rid herself of it.

Ultimately Jenny wanted to participate comfortably in staff meetings. But that goal was too vague. Instead, she defined her goal in more specific behavioral terms: to volunteer three comments at each staff meeting. She felt if she did that long enough, eventually she could speak up with ease.

Once her target was established, she broke it down into minigoals and included additional strategies and techniques to make achieving them easier.

Goal #1
Warm-ups
a. To practice relaxation before the staff meeting to help reduce physical tension.
b. To prepare for the meeting by reviewing the subject matter to be discussed.

With these two activities, Jenny increased her chances of feeling prepared and relaxed in the meeting.

Goal #2
a. To warm up with the relaxation and the review.
b. To volunteer one comment.

No standards were set for the quality of the comment. It could be as trivial as mentioning the date of an upcoming event. What mattered was that she volunteered *something*.

Goal #3
a. To warm up.
b. To volunteer two comments.

Goal #4
a. To warm up.
b. To volunteer three comments.

Jenny progressed from one goal to the next at her own pace. It took her several weeks to reach her target goal of three comments per meeting. After that, she continued to monitor her participation until her self-consciousness disappeared.

The very modesty of the goals and the simplicity of the strategy enabled a timid young woman to begin tackling a big assertion problem. Probably the most important outcome of this project was that it helped Jenny realize she could learn to manage her fears and control her behavior more effectively. Once she realized that she could walk into what seemed like a lion's den and speak up without being eaten alive, she became more optimistic about her ability to assert herself in other situations.

Jenny's change program illustrates some basic principles for modifying behavior:

1. Begin with a meaningful project, but one that isn't too urgent or too difficult. Although speaking up at staff meetings was hard for Jenny, it was less anxiety provoking than asserting herself to her roommate, her boyfriend, or her parents.
2. Goals should be defined as specifically as possible. Leave

abstractions to the philosophers. Jenny translated her desire to be more assertive into a very tangible target goal: to speak up three times at each staff meeting.

3. Tackle the project by starting with small, easy steps and progressing to increasingly difficult ones.

Jenny's project also demonstrates how additional strategies can be incorporated into the basic plan. After dividing her target into minigoals, Jenny added the warm-ups of relaxation and review. Had she been less anxious, she might have omitted the relaxation. The review was a good idea in any event. By stimulating her thinking, it made it easier to find something to say at the meeting.

This plan worked for Jenny. But if it hadn't, there are other strategies she could have tried. She might have monitored her self-talk before and during staff meetings in order to change self-defeating internal chatter. She could have made a contract and/or set up a reward system. Any number of combinations would have been possible.

Whereas Jenny wanted to *increase* her ease with self-assertion, Alexandra wanted to *decrease* the stress in her work life. A fifty-four-year-old divorced free-lance writer, Alexandra was in the seemingly enviable position of being wealthy. But financial independence is a double-edged sword for achievement-oriented women. It can help to create a sense of security that makes it easier to take risks. Or it can reduce motivation by removing the urgency of necessity. In Alexandra's case financial security permitted her to retreat from aggressively seeking work without suffering economic hardship.

Money, however, didn't spare her psychological distress. Alexandra felt frustrated by a large gap between her level of aspiration and her performance. She wanted to increase her productivity and to expand from local to national publications. But she wasn't doing much about it.

Her work life was characterized by tension, inefficiency, and avoidance.

Alexandra attempted to deal with her stress by practicing meditation, but found it didn't help her feel more confident. What emerged, after discussion, was that what had appeared to be one problem—stress—was in fact a collection of problems, which included faulty diet, self-assertion difficulties, poor work habits, and helpless self-talk. Since these are different types of problems requiring different types of solutions, no single strategy, such as meditation, could possibly solve them all. A more comprehensive approach was needed.

Alexandra started her self-management program by breaking down her target goal of decreasing stress into a series of minigoals. She began with the minigoal that was easiest for her: changing her diet. She substituted herbal tea for coffee. After only one week, she was considerably less nervous. She was so impressed by the dramatic effect of caffeine on her body that she began to wonder about the effect of alcohol. The next week she substituted mineral water for her dinner wine and found that her entire evening was transformed. Her increased energy added three productive hours to her day.

These dietary changes were a good opening number for Alexandra's self-management project because they were relatively easy for her. Giving up coffee and dinner wine involved neither a struggle with addiction nor a major sacrifice of pleasure. Her success in making these changes gave her energy and a sense of optimism with which to tackle more difficult minigoals.

Like many women, Alexandra had problems asserting herself in the realm of work. Specifically, she had difficulty presenting her work positively. But in addition to feeling the usual feminine inhibitions about bragging, she felt embarrassed by her limited productivity, and she discounted what she had actually accomplished. Since she felt her achievements were minimal, discussing them stirred up painful feelings of inadequacy. She longed to be swallowed up by the earth when people asked, "So, what have you been doing?" She responded with a few awkward words that made her feel terrible about herself and did little to promote her career. Since this type of question was asked repeatedly at professional gatherings, such gatherings were a nightmare for her and she avoided them. However, in avoiding fellow writers, she limited her access to information and opportunity.

Finding a good answer to the question "So, what have you been doing?" was Alexandra's next minigoal. What she did was quite simple. She broke the project down into two tasks: script writing and rehearsing. She made a list of all the articles she had published in the past two years and where she had published them. She memorized the list and then rehearsed it, making a special effort to recite it with an energetic and assured manner. And before she went out to network, she rehearsed it again. This simple strategy worked like a charm. It eliminated the black cloud of tension and awkwardness that hung over Alexandra's networking activities, freeing her to be sociable and to enjoy mingling with colleagues. In addition, by reviewing her accomplishments, Alexandra gained more respect for them and struck a blow against the feminine discounting habit.

Realizing that poor work habits create stress as well as inefficiency, Alexandra set about to tackle the disorganization in her work life. To begin with, her office was always a mess. The floor was covered with piles of books, magazines, and newspaper clippings; manuscripts, notes, and letters were scattered all over. Time management was equally chaotic. She worked only when the spirit moved her. When at work, she was constantly summoned to the phone by an active social life. Invariably, she dropped her work and chatted, while her answering machine remained hidden under an unsorted pile of papers. When actually working, Alexandra worked hard but not smart. She did extensive research, but always ended up with too many ideas and too little focus. She never outlined her material; she just sat down and started to write. Often she didn't finish articles because she couldn't decide what to cut.

To bring some order into her chaotic work life, Alexandra set several minigoals:

1. To manage the clutter, she would buy a file cabinet and a large worktable.
2. To improve time management, she would establish a work schedule of two hours, 9:00 A.M. to 11:00 A.M., come hell or high water, when she would plug in her answering machine.
3. To increase productivity and efficiency, she would train herself to create a detailed outline before she started writing.

These changes were simple but not easy. For a time it bothered her to ignore her phone—someone might need her. Establishing regular work hours after years of following momentary impulses was a challenge. And, at the beginning, her outlines were sketchy because she wasn't skilled at the decision-making process involved. But with practice the outlines became more detailed and eventually served as guides for her writing.

Alexandra's last minigoal was to modify the helpless thinking that undermined her productivity, efficiency, and morale. When sitting down to write, she frequently looked at her notes and thought, "This is a big jumble. I am never going to transform it into an article." Or "I can't really write. These ideas are silly. No one will want this." Too often she put off the work and lost touch with it, making it harder to resume at a later time. Using the strategies described in Chapter 9, she learned to counter her helpless thoughts with comments such as "Don't lynch the defendant; the jury is still out." Or "This is helpless thinking. Ignore it and get to work."

It took Alexandra over seven months to achieve her minigoals. Doing so didn't solve all her problems, but her confidence, efficiency, and productivity were increased, and her stress was decreased enormously. And she anticipated her first publication in a national magazine.

Alexandra's project gives us important pointers on how to decrease unwanted behavior:

1. Making major changes in behavior patterns, particularly entrenched habits, takes time. It rarely takes less than six weeks and often takes more than six months. Bring along plenty of patience.
2. What appears to be one big problem may be a *collection* of problems that need to be dealt with individually, often using very different types of strategies.
3. It's easier to eliminate unwanted behavior when we can substitute an alternative. The project of decreasing one habit translates into the project of increasing another. The goal of eliminating coffee becomes the goal of drinking herbal tea. The goal of decreasing helpless thinking becomes the goal of increasing productive self-talk.
4. When we want to change our behavior, it's tempting to try to change everything at once. We all know people who go on a health kick. One morning they get up and decide to lose weight, stop smoking, and start jogging. This isn't a good idea. Taking on too much is a setup for failure. It's better to tackle one goal at a time, to begin modestly and build on small successes.

Some behavior patterns require strategies and techniques beyond the scope of this book. Other behavior patterns are part of larger psychological problems, such as major anxiety or depression, which need the attention of trained mental health professionals. If you feel too stuck to give the self-help approach a serious try, or if you make a thoroughgoing attempt to take action and still can't get going, professional help is an option to consider.

These limitations notwithstanding, the practice of focusing, setting goals, and using an assortment of strategies to achieve those goals can take us a long way.

THE DOMINO THEORY

In trying to understand women's internal obstacles to achievement we found that many behavior patterns, in an assortment of combinations, can get in our way: the feminine discounting habit, learned helplessness, an inhibited mastery orientation, fear of failure, lack of assertion, and personal habits. It may seem like an uphill battle—even with strategies and techniques to help us. But the hill isn't as steep as it may look.

Imagine a row of dominoes. When dominoes are lined up, you don't have to tap each one individually to knock them all down. Since one stroke will do the trick, the job is simpler than it appears at first glance.

The same thing is true of behavior. Taking action in one area of one's life can bring about improvement in other areas. A woman who began applying to MBA programs, something she had wanted to do for a long time, found that her feelings about herself began to change. Her self-image blossomed and her self-esteem soared. She cut her hair, bought new clothes, and even felt sexier. As her perception of control increased, her horizons broadened and she discovered new interests and opportunities.

Taking action initiates an upward spiral. As we set goals, however modest, work toward them, and achieve them, we begin to learn that action pays off. We realize we can make things happen. The more we experience our impact, the more we feel inclined to set new goals, make more plans, and see them through to the finish. We get hooked.

As one woman put it, "The more I do, the more enthusiastic I get, and the more I want to do."

That's how we win the game. A few taps here, a few taps there. Before we know it, we have knocked down more dominoes than we ever dreamt possible.

Notes

Chapter 1

1. C. Tavris and A. J. Baumgartner, "How Would Your Life Be Different If You'd Been Born a Boy?" *Redbook* (1983) 160, 4:92–94.

2. See review in K. Deaux, *The Behavior of Women and Men* (Monterey, Calif.: Brooks/Cole, 1976).

3. V. C. Crandall, "Sex Differences in Expectancy of Intellectual and Academic Reinforcement," in R. K. Unger and F. L. Denmark, eds., *Woman: Dependent or Independent Variable?* (New York: Psychological Dimensions, 1975).

4. See review in Deaux, *Behavior of Women and Men.*

5. *Ibid.*

6. *Ibid.*

7. K. Deaux and T. Emswiller, "Explanations of Successful Performance on Sex-Linked Tasks: What Is Skill for the Male Is Luck for the Female," *Journal of Personality and Social Psychology* (1974) 29:80–85.

8. N. T. Feather and J. G. Simon, "Reactions to Male and Female Success and Failure in Sex-Linked Occupations," *Journal of Personality and Social Psychology* (1975) 31:20–31.

9. S. Feldman-Summers and S. B. Kiesler, "Those Who Are Number Two Try Harder: The Effect of Sex on Attributions of Causality," *Journal of Personality and Social Psychology* (1974) 39:846–855.

Chapter 2

1. M. E. P. Seligman, *Helplessness: On Depression, Development, and Death* (San Francisco: Freeman, 1975).

2. *Ibid.*

3. *Ibid.*

4. J. Ernest, *Mathematics and Sex* (Santa Barbara, Calif.: University of California, Ford Foundation reprint, 1976).

5. S. Kogelman, *Debilitating Mathematics Anxiety: Its Dynamics and Etiology*, unpublished master's essay, Smith College School of Social Work, 1975. See review in B. Donady, S. Kogelman, and S. Tobias, "Math Anxiety and Female Mental Health: Some Unexpected Links," in C. L. Heckerman, ed., *The Evolving Female: Women in a Psychosocial Context* (New York: Human Sciences Press, 1980).

6. E. Schildkamp-Kundinger, *Die Frauenrolle und die Mathematikleistung* (Düsseldorf: Schwann, 1974). See review in B. Donady et al., "Math Anxiety and Female Mental Health: Some Unexpected Links."

7. Ernest, *Mathematics and Sex*.

8. B. Donady et al., "Math Anxiety and Female Mental Health: Some Unexpected Links."

9. Attributed to Calvin Coolidge. See Robert Pritikin, *Christ Was an Ad Man: The Amazing New Testament in Advertising* (San Francisco: Harbor, 1980).

10. D. S. Hiroto, "Locus of Control and Learned Helplessness." *Journal of Experimental Psychology* (1974) 102:187–193.

11. H. Kurlander et al., "Learned Helplessness, Depression, and Prisoner's Dilemma," in Seligman, *Helplessness*.

12. Seligman, *Helplessness*.

13. C. I. Diener and C. S. Dweck, "An Analysis of Learned Helplessness," *Journal of Personality and Social Psychology* (1978) 36:451–462.

14. Research of J. M. Weiss, summarized in Seligman, *Helplessness*.

15. J. E. Hokanson et al., "Availability of Avoidance Behaviors in Modulating Vascular-Stress Responses," *Journal of Personality and Social Psychology* (1971) 19:60–68.

16. Seligman, *Helplessness*.

17. *Ibid*.

18. M. E. P. Seligman et al., "The Alleviation of Learned Helplessness in the Dog," *Journal of Abnormal and Social Psychology* (1968) 73:256–262.

Chapter 3

1. L. W. Hoffman, "Changes in Family Roles, Socialization, and Sex Differences," *American Psychologist* (1977) 32:644–657.

2. J. H. Block, J. Block, and D. Harrington, "Sex Role Typing and Instrumental Behavior," paper presented at the Society for Research in Child Development, 1975.

3. K. Day, *Differences in Teaching Behavior in Adults as a Function of Sex-Related Variables*, unpublished Ph.D. dissertation, University of Washington, 1975.

4. See review by M. Guttentag and H. Bray, "Teachers as Mediators of Sex Role Standards," in A. G. Sargent, ed., *Beyond Sex Roles* (St. Paul: West, 1977).

5. J. H. Block, *Personality Development in Males and Females: The Influence of Differential Socialization*, unpublished manuscript, University of California at Berkeley, 1979.

6. See review by C. Tavris and C. Offir, *The Longest War* (New York: Harcourt Brace Jovanovich, 1977).

7. Block, *Personality Development*.

8. *Ibid.*; M. E. P. Seligman, *Helplessness: On Depression, Development, and Death* (San Francisco: Freeman, 1975).

9. Block, *Personality Development*.

10. See review in Block, *Personality Development*.

11. *Ibid*.

12. See reviews in Guttentag and Bray, "Teachers As Mediators," and in Block, *Personality Development*.

13. Block, *Personality Development*.

14. *Ibid*.

15. D. C. Glass and J. E. Singer, *Urban Stress: Experi-*

ments on Noise and Social Stressors (New York: Academic Press, 1972).

16. Simone de Beauvoir, *The Second Sex* (New York: Knopf, 1952).

17. Hoffman, "Changes in Family Roles."

18. See review by L. W. Hoffman, "Early Childhood Experiences and Women's Achievement Motive," *Journal of Social Issues* (1972) 28, 2:129–155.

19. C. S. Dweck and B. G. Licht, "Learned Helplessness and Intellectual Achievement," in M. E. P. Seligman and J. Garber, eds., *Human Helplessness: Theory and Research* (New York: Academic Press, 1980).

20. Block, *Personality Development*.

21. *Ms.* magazine, January 1983.

22. M. Hennig and A. Jardim, *The Managerial Woman* (New York: Pocket Books, 1976).

Chapter 4

1. See review in A. H. Stein and M. M. Bailey, "The Socialization of Achievement Orientation in Females," *Psychological Bulletin* (1973) 80:345–366.

2. *Ibid.*

3. J. Kagan and H. Moss, *Birth to Maturity* (New York: Wiley, 1962).

4. C. S. Dweck and B. G. Licht, "Learned Helplessness and Intellectual Achievement," in M. E. P. Seligman and J. Garber, eds., *Human Helplessness: Theory and Research* (New York: Academic Press, 1980).

5. *Ibid.*

6. C. I. Diener and C. S. Dweck, "An Analysis of Learned Helplessness," *Journal of Personality and Social Psychology* (1978) 36:451–462.

7. *Ibid.*

8. *Ibid.*

9. *Ibid.*

10. *Ibid.*

Chapter 5

1. Pamela Butler, *Self-Assertion for Women* (San Francisco: Harper & Row, 1981).

2. G. M. Phillips and E. C. Erickson, *Interpersonal Dynamics in the Small Group* (New York: Random House, 1970).

3. See review in E. D. Gambrill and C. A. Richey, "Assertion Training for Women," in C. L. Heckerman, ed., *The Evolving Female: Women in a Psychosocial Context* (New York: Human Sciences Press, 1980).

4. K. Hall, *Sex Differences in Initiation and Influence in Decision-Making Groups of Prospective Teachers*, unpublished Ph.D. dissertation, Stanford University, 1972.

5. B. L. Harragan, *Games Mother Never Taught You: Corporate Gamesmanship for Women* (New York: Warner Books, 1977).

6. M. R. Leonard, *Assertiveness Training Needs of Professional Business Women*, unpublished paper, 1978, cited in C. L. Meuhlenhard, "Women's Assertion and the Feminine Sex-Role Stereotype," in V. Franks and E. D. Rothblum, eds., *The Stereotyping of Women: Its Effects on Mental Health* (New York: Springer, 1983).

7. E. Megargee, "Influence of Sex Roles on the Manifestation of Leadership," *Journal of Applied Psychology* (1969) 53:377–382.

8. See review in Meuhlenhard, "Women's Assertion."

9. J. B. Miller, *Toward a New Psychology of Women* (Boston: Beacon Press, 1976).

10. See review in Gambrill, "Assertion Training for Women."

11. A. J. Lange and P. Jakubowski, *Responsible Assertive Behavior: Cognitive/Behavioral Procedures for Trainers* (Champaign, Ill.: Research Press, 1976).

Chapter 7

1. Michael Korda, *Power: How to Get It, How to Use It* (New York: Random House, 1975).

2. See review by R. Janoff-Bulman and P. Brickman, "Expectations and What People Learn from Failure," in N. T. Feather, ed., *Expectations and Actions: Expectancy-Value Models in Psychology* (Hillsdale, N.J.: Erlbaum, 1982).

3. T. Presbrey, *Social Problem Solving: Impact and Effects of Training on a Normal Adult Population*, unpublished Ph.D. dissertation, University of Hawaii, 1979.

4. See review in D. L. Watson and R. G. Tharp, *Self-Directed Behavior: Self-Modification for Personal Adjustment* (Monterey, Calif.: Brooks/Cole, 1981).

Chapter 8

1. A. Lakein, *How to Get Control of Your Time and Your Life* (New York: New American Library, 1973).

2. C. Garfield, interviewed by R. Trubo, "Peak Performance," *Success: The Magazine for Achievers* (1983) 30, 4:30–33, 56.

3. See review in E. D. Gambrill and C. A. Richey, "Assertion Training for Women," in C. L. Heckerman, ed., *The Evolving Female: Women in a Psychosocial Context* (New York: Human Sciences Press, 1980).

4. D. E. Griffin and D. L. Watson, "A Written, Personal Commitment from the Student Encourages Better Course Work," *Teaching of Psychology* (1978) 5:155.

5. M. F. Vincent, "Comparison of Self-Concepts of College Women: Athletes and Physical Education Majors," *Research Quarterly* (1976) 47:218–225.

6. See review in R. L. Williams and J. D. Long, *Toward a Self-Managed Life Style* (Boston: Houghton Mifflin, 1979).

Chapter 9

1. Attributed to Dorothy Corkille Briggs. See L. S. Sanford and M. E. Donovan, *Women and Self-Esteem* (New York: Penguin, 1985).

2. D. C. Rimm and S. Litvak, "Self-Verbalization and Emotional Arousal," *Journal of Abnormal Psychology* (1969) 74: 181–187.

Index

About the Author

SUSAN SCHENKEL, PH.D., is a clinical psychologist who has published research on identity in women and has taught courses on the psychology of women at several colleges. She has also been a clinical instructor in the Department of Psychiatry at Harvard Medical School. She is now in private practice in Cambridge, Massachusetts, where she does personal counseling and consultation and gives workshops to business, professional, and educational groups.